UKRAINE AFTER SHELEST

edited by

Bohdan Krawchenko

Canadian Institute of Ukrainian Studies
University of Alberta
Edmonton   1983

THE CANADIAN LIBRARY IN UKRAINIAN STUDIES

A series of original works and reprints relating to Ukraine, issued under the editorial supervision of the Canadian Institute of Ukrainian Studies, University of Alberta, Edmonton.

Copyright © 1983   Canadian Institute of Ukrainian Studies
                    University of Alberta
                    Edmonton, Alberta, Canada

Canadian Cataloguing in Publication Data
   Ukraine after Shelest

      (The Canadian library in Ukrainian studies)
      Essays originally presented at a panel sponsored by the Canadian Institute of Ukrainian Studies, the Canadian Association of Slavists and the Canadian Political Science Association, organized during the May 1981 Learned Societies Conference held at Dalhousie University.
      ISBN 0-920862-26-8

1. Ukraine—Politics and government—1917—Addresses, essays, lectures. I. Krawchenko, Bohdan, 1946– II. Canadian Institute of Ukrainian Studies. III. Canadian Association of Slavists. IV. Canadian Political Science Association. V. Learned Societies Conference (1981: Dalhousie University) VI. Series.

DK508.8.U39   320.947'71   C83–091199–5

Cover design: Alexander Korenfeld

Printed in Canada by Printing Services, University of Alberta
Distributed by the   University of Toronto Press
                      5201 Dufferin St.
                      Downsview, Ontario
                      Canada M3H 5T8

Ukraine After Shelest

Contents

Preface

Petro Iu. Shelest was the first secretary of the Communist Party of Ukraine from 1963 until his demise in 1972. His tenure of office coincided with a period of rising social unrest, cultural turmoil and national assertiveness—processes which were reflected in the Ukrainian party. The mass arrests of Ukrainian dissidents and the dismissal of many party and state officials in the wake of Shelest's ouster represented an attempt to reverse the partial gains made during the 1960s. The central leadership in Moscow charged Volodymyr V. Shcherbytsky, the new first secretary of the Communist Party of Ukraine, with the task of returning Ukraine to a state of subservient 'normality'. The successes and failures of Shcherbytsky's mission represent the major theme of this collection of essays.

This volume emerged from a panel on contemporary Ukraine, sponsored by the Canadian Institute of Ukrainian Studies, the Canadian Association of Slavists and the Canadian Political Science Association, organized during the May 1981 Learned Societies Conference held at Dalhousie University, Halifax, Nova Scotia. The essays included are revised versions of papers presented at that time. Professors Bociurkiw, Daycock, Isajiw, Rozumny and Woroby who acted as commentators for the panel deserve special thanks; as do David Marples and Peter Matilainen of the Canadian Institute of Ukrainian Studies for their assistance in bringing out this volume.

Politics and the National Question in the Post-Shelest Period

Roman Solchanyk

The year 1972 marked a turning point in the postwar history of Ukraine. In January the Soviet security apparatus conducted widespread political arrests throughout the republic, and imprisoned many leading participants in the national and cultural revival that had begun to take shape during the previous decade. Four months later Petro Iu. Shelest was removed from his post as first secretary of the Communist Party of Ukraine; subsequently it became clear that Shelest was purged for a variety of sins that constituted a "deviation" from officially sanctioned Soviet nationalities policy.

These two events dramatically illustrate the focal point in any discussion of politics in Ukraine—i.e., the interrelationship, in terms of nationality issues, between the central party leadership in Moscow, its local organization in Kiev, and the national elites. It is within this framework, which is applicable to a greater or lesser degree in all the non-Russian republics of the USSR, that developments in Ukraine during the post-Shelest period are considered. Before proceeding further, it may be useful to discuss briefly the main features of Soviet nationalities policy in the years preceding Shelest's dismissal and the circumstances surrounding his fall.

Most Western observers agree that the assumption of power by Brezhnev and his colleagues in October 1964 was followed by a re-evaluation of the assimilationist policies of the latter years of Khrushchev's rule. Specifically, it is argued that the new leadership retreated from the merger (*sliianie*) of nations formula characteristic of Soviet nationalities policy in the early 1960s.[1] The term was not used by Brezhnev in his Central Committee report to the first post-Khrushchev congress of the Communist Party of the Soviet Union (CPSU) in 1966, nor was it to be found in the speeches of party leaders and in official documents generated by the celebration of the fiftieth anniversary of the October Revolution in 1967. According to one scholar, the explicit acknowledgement that the merger of nations was "no longer operative" was signalled by an editorial in *Kommunist* in September 1969.[2]

Confirmation of this view may also be found in Soviet sources. M. I. Kulychenko (Kulichenko), a Ukrainian historian who since 1967 has headed the Sector of Theory of Nations and Nationality Relations of the Department of Scientific Communism in the Institute of Marxism-Leninism in Moscow, argues that

> It is no secret that in the beginning of the 1960s the literature exaggerated the results that had been achieved in drawing together (*sblizhenie*) of nations; individual scholars manifested nihilism in their interpretation of the national factor of the life of peoples and even began to search for ways to the merger (*sliianie*) of nations in the "foreseeable" future.[3]

It must be emphasized, however, that the *concept* of merger did not disappear from the theoretical arsenal of Soviet nationalities policy. Although it is not customarily referred to in the pronouncements of party leaders and in official party documents,[4] the merger of nations continues to be discussed in the specialized literature on the national question. As a rule, leading Soviet experts on nationality relations agree that merger is a process that will occur in the undetermined future when communism is established on a universal scale. Characteristic is the view of I. P. Tsamerian, senior scientific associate of the Institute of Philosophy of the USSR Academy of Sciences, that "the merger of nations is a world-wide process, not a local one. It cannot be attained within the framework of a single country (even such a powerful and multinational country as the USSR) or a group of countries."[5] According to another source, "the merger [of nations] is the disappearance of the qualitative characteristics of nations as communities of people. Merger, the disappearance of these historical communities...is a matter of the far distant future. And at the present time we cannot envision in detail how this disappearance will occur."[6] To this we might add the authoritative voice of P. N. Fedoseev, vice-president of the USSR Academy of Sciences, who reassures us that Lenin never viewed the merger of nations in terms of the elimination of national distinctions, but rather as a closer unity of socialist nations. Lenin argued, says Fedoseev, "that national distinctions will still be maintained for a very long time, even after the attainment of the dictatorship of the proletariat on a universal scale."[7] But although the general trend has been to downgrade the merger of nations as an operative principle, its proponents are still to be found within the Soviet academic community and, presumably, in the party.[8]

An indication of the Brezhnev leadership's initial concern about nationality issues was the decision, taken in May 1965, to conduct a scholarly discussion of the problem "On the Concept of 'Nation'" in the journal *Voprosy istorii*.[9] The articles that appeared in the symposium underlined the basic division among Soviet scholars between advocates and opponents of merger. In the final analysis, the party struck a balance of sorts by opting for the formula of the simultaneous and mutually interdependent process of the flourishing (*rastsvet*) and drawing together (*sblizhenie*) of nations, wherein the former is said to be promoted on the basis of the latter and vice versa. This process is understood in terms of a "dialectical unity of two tendencies," with the leading role ascribed to drawing together.[10]

In a parallel development, there emerged by the end of the 1960s another theoretical construct that implied a hardening of the official line toward the nationalities—i.e., the concept of the Soviet people (*sovetskii narod*). This idea had previously been articulated by Khrushchev in his report to the Twenty-second Congress of the CPSU in 1961, but was not included in either the draft or the final version of the new party programme adopted by the congress.[11] Nonetheless, in the ensuing years it became the subject of varied interpretations with radically different implications for the future development of nations in the USSR. In the 1969 *Kommunist* editorial mentioned earlier, the "Soviet multinational people" was described as a "new historical community" and a "remarkable expression of the international unity and equality of the Soviet socialist nations and nationalities."[12] The following year it was given fuller expression in the Central Committee's theses on the hundredth anniversary of Lenin's birth: "The Soviet people is a fundamentally new, international community of people, a socialist union of all the toilers of the USSR—workers in industry, agriculture, and culture, those engaged in physical and mental labour, who constitute the social base of the multinational state of all the people."[13] According to Soviet experts, the final phase of what might be termed the legitimization of the Soviet people formula was its formal announcement by Brezhnev at the Twenty-fourth Congress of the CPSU in 1971.[14]

If we look at the course of developments in Ukraine during this period, we find that trends that were set in motion as a result of the destalinization policies of the mid-1950s were gaining momentum and invariably moving along a collision course with the increasingly conservative and integrative policies of the Brezhnev leadership. It was at this time that Ukrainian literature and art experienced a national revival that was reflected in the works of the younger generation of writers, literary critics and artists collectively known as the *shestydesiatnyky*. They were concerned mainly with the fate of the Ukrainian language and culture, and sought increasingly more uninhibited expression in the press, at public meetings, and in the uncensored *samvydav* literature.[15] Initiated by the literati, the movement for national renaissance found supporters within all segments of the creative intelligentsia as well as among representatives of the technical elites. Valentyn Moroz, the well-known Ukrainian dissident who was allowed to emigrate to the West in 1979, provides an insight into the hopes and expectations of these young idealists and reformers:

> Actually, this generation—these were people who no longer had to think about bread, about salvation from hunger, as was the case in the 1933. This was a young generation that went into the universities, that could already think about something other than the elementary bases of existence. And, indeed, only these kind of people could sense that they were living in squalor (*u bahni*). Chornovil, for example, was editor of a Komsomol republican newspaper; Dziuba was one of the most important critics in the Ukrainian Writers' Union; and Stus was a postgraduate student at the Institute of Literature in Kiev. In short, these were people at the highest levels. They were talented, they had futures, they could have gone far in the communist establishment. But these were the best people in the moral sense, in the sense of moral qualities. They understood that to advocate that which one does not believe in, to simply advance one's career, to look on while one's nation is being russified—that this is squalor. That is, there emerged within these people the natural desire to free themselves of this squalor.[16]

In Moroz's words, the *shestydesiatnyky* were artists who wished to paint, but not only portraits of Lenin; they were poets who wanted to write, but not only about Stalin and peace; and they were scholars who wanted to conduct research and not simply produce what was ordered from above. They were bodies, says Moroz, in search of souls.

The intriguing question, of course, is to what extent such aspirations were supported by elements within the Communist Party of Ukraine and Shelest himself. Certainly in the 1960s much was done to counter the long-standing official ukrainophobia inspired by Stalin. The study of Ukrainian history was encouraged and new journals were established for this purpose. Journalists could publish articles that reflected pride in things Ukrainian without fear of reprisals as "enemies of Soviet power." According to *samvydav* sources, by the summer of 1965 plans were under way to reform the system of higher education in the republic with a view toward replacing Russian as the language of instruction with Ukrainian. None of this could have been possible without the approval of the party leadership in Kiev.[17] Of interest here is the concern expressed by the Moscow *samvydav* publication *Politicheskii dnevnav* in June 1965 about the intensification of "nationalist tendencies" in Ukraine, which were also said to have been "reflected in the activity of some state and even party organs."[18] This would seem to confirm the widely-held view that during the Shelest period the reform-minded intelligentsia was backed by influential segments of the Ukrainian party and government establishment.

The question of Shelest's role in this complex nexus of relationships between Moscow, Kiev and the national elites is much more difficult to answer. Those who are inclined to view Shelest as a latter-day national communist cite his various public statements in favour of developing the Ukrainian language and culture to support their view of the Ukrainian party leader as an "autonomist."[19] Conversely, one could easily assemble appropriate quotations from Shelest's speeches to portray him as a fairly typical product of the Soviet party apparatus. The truth probably lies somewhere in between and is perhaps reflected in the statement attributed to Shelest to the effect that he was not Lazar Kaganovich and these were not the times of Stalin.[20] Nevertheless, it was Shelest's misfortune to have presided over the Ukrainian party organization at a time when the canonization of the Soviet people formula effectively ruled out the further development of Ukrainian national identity of the 1960s—i.e., outside the framework of official nationalities policy. This "model" of conflicting concepts about nationality issues between the centre and the periphery is explained by party ideologists in the following manner:

> Under the conditions of Soviet reality, national self-awareness develops on the basis of the Marxist-Leninist world view, understanding the community of interests of all the peoples of the USSR, and the formation of international-patriotic feelings of the toilers. The attempt to represent national self-awareness apart from the common international tasks, to limit it to the narrow concepts of national interests and needs degenerates into a position of nationalism.[21]

This same author cites the case of Shelest as a concrete example of precisely such a conflict of views on nationality issues.[22] Clearly, this does not preclude the existence of a multiplicity of factors that ultimately may have contributed to Shelest's downfall.[23] It does, however, reject the contention that foreign policy issues played a leading role in the Shelest affair,[24] and focuses instead on the national question as the primary consideration in Ukrainian politics.[25]

In the years since Shelest's fall, the Ukrainian party leadership under Volodymyr V. Shcherbytsky has proven to be a reliable instrument in the implementation of Soviet nationalities policy. This policy casts Ukrainians in the role of younger brothers or junior partners to the Russians, under whose leadership Soviet society is to attain the unity that is clearly implicit in the concept of the Soviet people. However, unlike the 1954 message of the 300th anniversary of Ukraine's "reunification" with Russia, which suggested a distinct identity for Ukrainians in the Russo-Ukrainian relationship, the recent celebrations of the 325th anniversary of the Pereiaslav Agreement and the 1500th anniversary of Kiev point to an unmistakable shift in the direction of greater integration.[26] This trend appears to bear out John Armstrong's view, expressed some years ago, that the major thrust of Soviet nationalities policy would be directed at "drawing the younger brothers (especially the Ukrainians) into indissoluble junior partnership with the Russians as the dominant ethnic group."[27] The crucial question, of course, is how far the regime is willing to go in pursuit of this *Gleichschaltung*. Shcherbytsky, the central figure charged with translating this policy into reality, has shown that, unlike Shelest, he has no reservations about fulfilling his tasks. In a recent interview, when asked to describe how the Ukrainian party "works as part of the Communist Party of the Soviet Union," he answered:

> In all of its practical work, the Communist Party of the Ukraine proceeds, as ever, from the general party program documents and works under the leadership of the Central Committee of the Communist Party of the Soviet Union. Communists of the republic take an active part in drawing up the policy, strategy and tactic (*sic*) of the party at CPSU congresses and at the plenums of its Central Committee. *The Communist Party of the Ukraine organizes all the work in implementing the policy of the CPSU within the republic.*[28] (Emphasis added)

Indeed, the question of implementation of CPSU policies is the central problem confronting all republican party leaders. It is a problem that Shelest could not resolve to Moscow's satisfaction, but one which Shcherbytsky has thus far mastered.

The purging of Shelest and the various personnel changes in the party and government that accompanied his removal from the Ukrainian political scene have been adequately treated elsewhere.[29] However, we will summarize briefly the main developments in party politics since 1972, focusing on those issues that remain problematic, while placing primary emphasis on recent trends in the republic, particularly after the Twenty-fifth Congress of the Communist Party of Ukraine in 1976.

When was the move against Shelest actually initiated, by whom, and on what basis? Even partial answers to these questions might provide insights into the specific circumstances surrounding the purge of Shelest and, more broadly, permit a better understanding of the nature of politics in Ukraine.

Most observers view the appointment of V. V. Fedorchuk to replace V. F. Nikitchenko as chief of the Ukrainian KGB in July 1970 as a clear indication of Shelest's impending troubles. This perception is almost certainly correct, particularly since the ties between Shelest and Nikitchenko go back to the mid-1920s.[30] Nonetheless, the drive against Shelest may have been launched already in early 1968 in connection with the campaign that was organized in Dnipropetrovsk against Oles Honchar's novel, *Sobor*. Honchar, by virtue of his position as first secretary of the Board of the Ukrainian Writers' Union, symbolized the cultural policies associated with Shelest. Moreover, he is said to have been personally close to the Ukrainian party leader.[31] Significantly, the most acute criticism of Honchar, including an attack in the all-Union press by A. A. Ulanov, first secretary of the Dnipropetrovsk city party committee,[32] was mobilized by the Dnipropetrovsk party organization headed by O. F. Vatchenko—i.e., by associates of Brezhnev and Shcherbytsky.[33] Vatchenko is also the only party functionary from Ukraine known to have spoken at the 19 May 1972 plenum of the CPSU Central Committee that removed Shelest from his post.

The first important personnel change following Shcherbytsky's installment as Ukrainian party leader was the replacement of Shelest's Central Committee secretary for ideology, F. D. Ovcharenko, by V. Iu. Malanchuk at the 10 October 1972 plenum of the Central Committee.[34] Shcherbytsky's choice of Malanchuk—a scholar-apparatchik thoroughly versed in nationality issues, with previous experience in ideological work in the sensitive Lviv oblast, and a solid reputation as a hard-line "russifier"—supports the thesis that the national question, a paramount ideological problem, was at the root of Shelest's troubles in Ukraine.[35] During the next two years Malanchuk supervised a broad purge of the republic's political and cultural institutions. As Grey Hodnett points out, the purge took an especially heavy toll of cadres in the ideological-cultural sector, which once again emphasizes what lay behind Shelest's ouster.[36] Among important party functionaries, V. M. Terletsky was replaced as chief editor of *Komunist Ukrainy* in November 1972 by V. F. Sokurenko;[37] V. V. Tsvietkov was removed as head of the Science and Educational Institutions Department at the end of 1972 in favour of F. M. Rudych;[38] I. Z. Orel was succeeded as head of the Propaganda and Agitation Department on 15 October 1973 by Iu. N. Ielchenko;[39] and P. M. Fedchenko was replaced as head of the Culture Department by M. H. Ishchenko at the end of 1973.[40] In addition, in 1973, V. I. Zahorodny replaced A. T. Chekaniuk as rector of the Higher Party School,[41] and the following year I. D. Nazarenko was succeeded as director of the Institute of Party History by V. I. Iurchuk.[42] Other personnel shifts bearing directly on cultural and educational affairs were the replacement of Iurii Smolych as chairman of the Board of the Writers' Union by Vasyl Kozachenko (who was elected first secretary) at the fourth plenum of the Writers' Union on 23 March 1973,[43] and the retirement of Iu. N. Dadenkov, at the age of sixty-two, from his position as minister of higher and secondary specialized education on 13 November 1973 in favour of H. H. Iefimenko.[44]

Not all the personnel changes of 1972–4 were clearly related to the Shelest affair. Nazarenko, for example, was sixty-four when he left his post as director of the Institute of Party History, after having held that position since 1956. Although his early association with Kharkiv suggests a link to Shelest, it is not inconceivable that he simply retired after seventeen years of service. The dismissal of V. I. Degtiarev, first secretary of the Donetsk oblast party committee, in December 1975, was widely interpreted as Shcherbytsky's "final victory" against Shelest's supporters, largely on the premise that Shcherbytsky later criticized Shelest and Degtiarev by name and in the same breath at the Twenty-sixth Congress of the Ukrainian party.[45] Yet this argument ignores the nature of the criticism levelled by Shcherbytsky against Degtiarev at the Donetsk oblast party conference in January 1976 and then at the party congress itself—i.e., *inter alia*, cadres policy. Nor does it take into account the testimony of *Ukrainskyi visnyk* that Degtiarev, Vatchenko and V. F. Dobryk were overt enemies of Shelest.[46] Similarly, it has been argued that the removal of V. I. Shynkaruk from the editorial board of *Komunist Ukrainy* in April 1973 (together with Tsvietkov, H. H. Shevel, and Z. P. Shulha) was purge-related.[47] Yet, the fact that Shynkaruk has continued to hold the highly sensitive position of director of the Institute of Philosophy from 1968 until the present day belies this interpretation.[48]

The length of time between Shcherbytsky's assumption of power and the removal of certain persons raises some interesting questions. First, as Yaroslav Bilinsky notes, it suggests that Shcherbytsky encountered serious difficulties in consolidating his power over the Ukrainian party organization after Shelest's removal. Another possibility, put forward by Hodnett, is that some personnel changes may have been related to problems other than the Shelest purge:

> The stretching out of these personnel changes, of course, raises the question of whether one is dealing with a process motivated by a *single* intention to effect a pattern of purging, or with a more complex process of telescoping campaigns geared not only to the liquidation of Shelest's network of clients, supporters, and beneficiaries, but to subsequent campaigns, inability to implement policies, or new factionalism in the post-Shelest period.[49]

An excellent case in point is the transfer of V. S. Kutsevol from the position of first secretary of the Lviv oblast party committee to head the Committee of People's Control on 28 November 1973, and the election of Dobryk, a member of the Dnipropetrovsk group, in his place.[50] The length of time for Kutsevol's removal is puzzling. Dissident sources maintain that his dismissal was demanded by CPSU Central Committee secretary Suslov as early as the November 1971 plenum of the CPSU Central Committee. It was reportedly only Shelest's intercession on behalf of Kutsevol that delayed his ouster.[51]

Finally, how are we to explain the fates of certain persons whose comings and goings offer no ready explanation in the context of the Shelest purge? Ulanov, for example, author of the aforementioned article criticizing Honchar, was installed as head of the important Organizational Party Work Department sometime between April and August 1970.[52] This suggests that he was meant to play an important role in cadres work during the anti-Shelest campaign. Yet, on 25 July 1972, shortly after Shelest's removal, he was transferred to the post of secretary of the Voroshylovhrad oblast party committee and is now serving as Soviet ambassador to Liberia.[53] What happened? In some instances conclusive judgments are difficult to make.

Moving from individual cases to an analysis of the overall impact of the purge, one must consider Hodnett's suggestion that the purge, at least at the level of the top leadership, was less devastating than might have been expected.[54] Certainly, it seems that the contentions of *Ukrainskyi visnyk* that "the purge of party cadres in Ukraine was numerically the highest in the USSR" and that "it is comparable only to the purges of the 1930s" are exaggerated.[55] Bilinsky has attempted a statistical analysis of the membership of the Ukrainian party organization between 1971 and 1976, but on the basis of incomplete and confusing data.[56] In the meantime, the most recent edition of the official history of the Ukrainian party states that 37,000 party members—1.5 per cent of the total membership on 1 January 1973—were purged during the exchange of party cards in 1973 and 1974.[57] Nonetheless, there is little doubt that the purge had a significant qualitative impact, particularly in the related fields of ideology, culture and education. This is especially true if, in addition to those Ukrainian academics, writers, journalists and other representatives of the cultural intelligentsia who were arrested and tried in the course of 1972–3, one considers those who were treated in a relatively "liberal" fashion by being dismissed from their positions and spiritually, if not physically, isolated from the remainder of society.

The repression of Ukrainian cultural elites was accompanied by a broad ideological campaign that was particularly strident between 1972 and 1974. It centred on "deviations" in the social sciences and humanities, particularly in the fields of history, philosophy and literature.[58] The basis for this campaign was the editorial attack on Shelest's book *Ukraino nasha Radianska* (1970) in the April 1973 issue of *Komunist Ukrainy.*[59] Myroslav Prokop's assertion that the criticism of Shelest's book was aimed less at the author than at the cultural and historical values that define Ukrainian national identity is hardly disputable.[60] Why indeed should Shelest have been criticized when his fate had already been sealed in May 1972?

After the Twenty-fifth Congress of the Communist Party of Ukraine, a degree of stability unknown since Shelest's fall characterized republican politics. That stability was abruptly shattered with the announcement that the 26 April 1979 plenum of the Central Committee had decided to release Malanchuk from his position as candidate member of the Politburo and Central Committee secretary of ideology "in connection with his transfer to other work."[61] This move, which could only have been made in concert with higher authorities in Moscow, is the most important personnel change to have occurred in the Ukrainian party in recent years, and merits closer scrutiny, especially concerning the party's motives in the area of nationalities policy.

Malanchuk's removal as head of the republic's ideological apparatus came as a complete surprise largely because there had been little to suggest serious failures or shortcomings in ideological work in Ukraine. An assessment of this change is complicated further by the CPSU Central Committee's adoption, on the same day that Malanchuk was dismissed, of a decree "On the Further Improvement of Ideological, Political, and Educational Work"—the most comprehensive such statement since the Twenty-fifth Congress.[62] Thus, although the state of ideological work in the Soviet Union generally was being discussed in Moscow at about the time of Malanchuk's transfer, there is no clear direct link between the two developments. Shcherbytsky's comments at the 7–8 June meeting of the republic party's *aktiv*, which assembled in Kiev to discuss the all-Union ideological decree, provide little clarification. The Ukrainian party leader noted that there "exists a healthy ideological situation in the republic" for which he credited, in part, the scientific and cultural intelligentsia. The only passage in his speech that can be interpreted as a reflection on Malanchuk's work concerns the "very serious" tasks posed by the ideological decree:

> And we need to examine whether all our ideological cadres—from agitators up to the republican level—are capable of reorienting their work with a view toward the new demands. Obviously, not all of them will be able to do so. And concerning those who lag hopelessly behind, who are infected with formalism, and who either cannot or will not turn over a new leaf—we have to get rid of these workers as quickly as possible.[63]

One thing, however, is certain: Malanchuk departed from the Ukrainian political scene in disgrace. This is attested to, above all, by his non re-election to the Central Committee at the Twenty-sixth Congress of the Ukrainian party in February 1981.[64] In addition to being relieved of his party posts, on 27 June 1979 the Ukrainian Supreme Soviet stripped Malanchuk of his position as head of the Supreme Soviet's Commission on Foreign Affairs.[65] Moreover, Malanchuk was not included in the appropriate volume of the second edition of the *Ukrainska radianska entsyklopediia* published in 1981, although his biographies had previously appeared both in the three-volume *Ukrainskyi radianskyi entsyklopedychnyi slovnyk* (1966–8) and the four-volume *Radianska entsyklopediia istorii Ukrainy* (1969–72). However, his status as an expert on nationality relations has apparently remained intact. In late 1981 it was reported that Malanchuk participated in a scientific-theoretical conference in Makhachkala (Daghestan ASSR) devoted to the theme "The Twenty-sixth Congress of the CPSU and the Development of Nationality Relations in the USSR." Later it was learned that in June 1981 he delivered a paper at a session of the authoritative Scientific Council on Nationality Problems of the USSR Academy of Sciences. This latter source also identified him as an associate of the Kiev Polytechnical Institute.[66] These appear to be the first and thus far the only references to the former Ukrainian ideological chief in the Soviet press since his demise.

On 3 July 1979, not long after Malanchuk's dismissal, O. M. Marynych was removed as minister of education and replaced by M. V. Fomenko.[67] Shcherbytsky had criticized Marynych at the aforementioned meeting of party activists in connection with the need to raise the level of ideological work with the republic's youth:

> The republic's Ministry of Education, as well as several of its scientific-research institutes, have been dilatory in improving educational work. Their analysis of the real processes that are taking place in the life of the school are poor and their study and dissemination of advanced experience is unsatisfactory. Unfortunately, the leadership of the Ministry of Education (O. M. Marynych) is not drawing the [proper] conclusions from criticism and is working as before.[68]

Shcherbytsky chastised the newspaper *Radianska osvita* and its editor, S. P. Zalovoka, who was removed from the editorial board after 13 June. This combination of events suggests that the dismissals of Malanchuk and Marynych were related. A plausible scenario is that the renewed emphasis on the teaching of Russian in the non-Russian republics, which reached new heights at the all-Union conference on "The Russian Language—the Language of Friendship and Co-operation of the Peoples of the USSR," held in Tashkent on 22–24 May 1979, provided the political matrix for both demotions.[69] A more viable hypothesis, however, based on an overall view of recent cultural policy in Ukraine, is that Malanchuk's ouster as chief arbiter of ideological affairs was engineered in an entirely different context—i.e., as part of an attempt to reach a working accommodation with the Ukrainian cultural intelligentsia.

The party's policy in this area has been to severely repress those elements unwilling to compromise their positions—e.g., the Ukrainian

Helsinki Group,[70] while at the same time offering others the possibility of returning to the fold. Thus, in the course of 1977 and in early 1978 the Soviet Ukrainian press published a number of statements by dissident intellectuals that, in varying degree, represented a *modus vivendi* with the regime. Among those who opted for this course were Hryhorii Kochur, Viktor Ivanysenko, Vasyl Zakharchenko, Volodymyr Sirenko, Hryhorii Avrakhov and Matvii Shestopal.[71] This process was by no means simple. Thus, although Mykhailo Braichevsky, author of *Pryiednannia chy vozziednannia?*, issued a statement in April 1972 protesting the publication of his essay abroad and claiming that he had never been persecuted for his scholarly beliefs or convictions, it was apparently not until the end of 1977 that he was once again permitted to publish.[72] Braichevsky's works are cited in Soviet historical publications,[73] but he has remained outside the academic establishment. Particularly revealing is his conspicuous absence from the various preparations for the May 1982 celebration of the 1500th anniversary of the city of Kiev. Similarly, although Kochur's translations and articles are now published occasionally, Dmytro Pavlychko did not even mention the dean of Ukrainian translators at the most recent congress of Ukrainian writers.[74] The latest handbook on writers in Ukraine reveals that Kochur has thus far not been re-admitted to the Ukrainian Writers' Union.[75]

Indications of a trend toward "cultural detente" in Ukraine have been apparent in a number of areas. In the literary field, several organizational changes of the past few years could only be greeted with approval by Ukrainian writers. These include the removal of Mykola Shamota from the position of director of the Institute of Literature in March 1978 and his replacement by Ihor Dzeverin;[76] Vasyl Kozachenko's transfer from the position of first secretary of the Board of the Ukrainian Writers' Union in January 1979 in favour of Pavlo Zahrebelny;[77] and the passing of Iurii Zbanatsky from the position of first secretary of the Kiev writers' organization in December 1980 and his replacement by Iurii Mushketyk.[78] Shamota, Kozachenko and Zbanatsky were all associated with the repression of their colleagues in the 1960s and 1970s. Also interesting is the change in the editorial staff of *Literaturna Ukraina* in March 1980, which witnessed the replacement of Vitalii Vynohradsky as chief editor by Petro Perebyinis.[79] Vynohradsky, a long-time party functionary, was appointed chief editor in June 1975 when he was not even a member of the Writers' Union.[80] His departure appears to have been greeted with a sigh of relief even by the party grouping of the Kiev writers' organization. Thus, at an open meeting of party members of the organization in July 1980, reference was made to "an improvement in the creative atmosphere in the editorial board of *Literaturna Ukraina*."[81] This sentiment was repeated by the young writer Volodymyr Iavorivsky, who remarked at the recent writers' congress that "the normal breathing of *Literaturna Ukraina* has been restored."[82] The same gathering witnessed a remarkable speech by Perebyinis, who emphasized "the national spirit and national character" of the writer's craft, and warned against "the violation of the balance, in one direction or the other, of the national in form and socialist in content formula that governs Soviet cultural policies."[83]

Another positive development has been the re-emergence of a number of writers previously harassed or persecuted because of their dissident activities or unorthodox writings. Among them are Roman Andriiashyk, Ivan Bilyk, Roman Ivanychuk, Borys Kharchenko, Mykhailo Kosiv, Mykola Lukash, Volodymyr Malyk and Stanislav Telniuk. In 1981 the Molod publishing house issued a collection of Vasyl Symonenko's poetry and prose entitled *Lebedi materynstva*, which had been scheduled for publication in 1972.[84] Perhaps one of the most significant developments has been Lina Kostenko's return to print with the publication of her *Nad berehamy vichnoi riky* (1977), *Marusia Churai* (1979) and *Nepovtornist* (1980), and her nomination for the 1981 Shevchenko State Prize for literature.[85] Evidence of the party's willingness to court the literary intelligentsia is also apparent in other areas.[86] Would this have been possible without the removal of Malanchuk, the chief architect of the post-Shelest cultural purge? Zahrebelny's statement at the Twenty-sixth Congress of the CPU that "a particularly favourable atmosphere has been created in the republic after the strengthening of the leadership of ideological sectors" is revealing.[87] In Soviet parlance the phrase "strengthening the leadership" refers to a purge of cadres. Evidently the dismissal of Malanchuk was the price demanded by the Ukrainian cultural elite for faithful co-operation in the further "building of communism." This view is reinforced by the results of the 4 November 1981 meeting, between the Ukrainian party and government leadership and representatives of the cultural intelligentsia, convened by the Politburo to discuss various aspects of cultural development in Ukraine. Shcherbytsky's speech was particularly warm, emphasizing the party's concern for Ukrainian cultural life and its readiness to lend a helping hand. "A sensible proposal and initiative," he assured his listeners, "always has found and will continue to find support." One after another, representatives of the creative unions addressed the gathering to plead the case of their special interest group. Among the proposals put forth were the transformation of the literary almanac *Kyiv* into a regular periodical; the creation of an Institute of Cinema and Television to train personnel in the film industry; and the establishment of a children's musical theatre in Kiev.[88] In short, the proceedings had all the characteristics of a marketplace where goods and services are exchanged for the right price.

The social sciences were especially hard hit by the post-Shelest purge. Signs of dissatisfaction with the work of Ukrainian historians, particularly in Lviv, were already apparent in 1971.[89] Throughout 1972 and 1973 such writers as Raisa Ivanchenko (Ivanova), Mykola Kytsenko, Leonid Makhnovets, Volodymyr Zaremba, Andriiashyk, Bilyk, Malyk and Zahrebelny were criticized for "distortions" in their treatment of past events and historical figures. In February 1972 F. P. Shevchenko was removed as chief editor of *Ukrainskyi istorychnyi zhurnal* and replaced as director of the Institute of Archeology.[90] The following month major personnel changes were made in the composition of the journal's editorial board, including changes of both deputy editors and the addition of seven new names to the staff.

The sharpest criticism of Ukrainian social scientists was unleashed at approximately the same time as the attack on Shelest's book in *Komunist Ukrainy*. At the general meeting of the Academy of Sciences' Division of Economics, History, Philosophy and Law on 12 March 1973, the Institutes of History, Archeology and Philosophy were singled out for publishing works that "idealized the past" and Ukrainian historians were rebuked for lagging behind in research on the development of the Soviet people.[91] Several days later Shcherbytsky, speaking at a meeting of the activists of the Kiev oblast and city party organizations, pointed out the "serious shortcomings" in the work of the Institute of Archeology, the Institute of Philosophy, and the Society for the Preservation of Historical and Cultural Monuments.[92] He also noted the problem of "idealization of the past" and lack of ideological steadfastness and party-mindedness among Ukrainian social scientists in his speech at the April 1973 plenum of the Central Committee:

> Mistakes and shortcomings in ideological work were criticized at the party activists' meetings that were recently held in the oblasts. Specifically, it was noted that in a number of publications there were deviations from class and party criteria in evaluating social phenomena and processes. Their authors manifested national conceit and narrow-mindedness, idealized the patriarchal way of life, and elucidated the historical past of the Ukrainian people from the ideologically fallacious position of "uniqueness" (*samobutnosti*). Certain authors presented a distorted version of the struggle for Ukraine's re-unification with Russia, the events of the October Revolution and Civil War, and the socialist reconstruction of society.[93]

At a general meeting of party members of the Kiev writers' organization on 22 October 1973, Malanchuk emphasized the need for an "objective class evaluation" of such historical figures as M. Drahomanov, M. Kostomarov, M. Skrypnyk and V. Blakytny, noting that in some books and articles they had been portrayed in a false light.[94] Shcherbytsky returned to this theme at the May 1974 plenum of the Central Committee, urging that the Institute of Party History play a more significant role in research in the social sciences.[95] Subsequently he announced that the Politburo had taken measures to broaden the Institute's leadership role as the co-ordinator of the development of the social sciences in the republic.[96]

The impact of these developments on Ukrainian historical studies was nothing short of catastrophic, and was reflected in the suppression of historical publications, the restructuring of scholarly institutions, dismissals from institutes and universities, and the appointment of party watchdogs to leading positions in academic institutions.[97] In 1972–3 the serial publications *Istorychni dzherela ta ikh vykorystannia; Istoriohrafichni doslidzhennia v Ukrainskii RSR; Mynule i suchasne Bukovyny; Ukrainskyi istoryko-heohrafichnyi zbirnyk; Seredni viky na Ukraini;* and *Kyivska starovyna* all ceased publication.[98] Numerous historical works, including such fundamental projects as the multi-volume publication of the archive of the Zaporozhian Sich, never saw the light of day.[99] The Institute of Philosophy and its journal *Filosofska dumka* abandoned historical research and, in the words of its director, "paid particular attention to deepening the ties between theoretical research and the policies of our party, the practice of communist construction, and especially the tasks of communist and international upbringing of the toilers." To that end two new departments were established in the institute: the Department of Scientific Communism and the Department of Theoretical Problems of National Relations and Proletarian Internationalism.[100] The Institute of Social Sciences disbanded one department and formed three others, including the Department of Criticism of the Ideology and Policies of Anti-Communism.[101] The institute's director, M. M. Oleksiuk, reported to the 1973 General Assembly of the Academy of Sciences in Kiev that

> in preceding years the scientific themes [at the institute] were largely geared to the past and weakly tied to the present. Recently a great deal has been done to bring them closer to the present and to the tasks of communist construction.... The problem of the struggle against the ideology and policies of anti-communism—first of all against Ukrainian bourgeois nationalism—is being worked on by all of the institute's departments.[102]

This was probably Oleksiuk's last major act as director of the institute, a post that he had held since 1963. In 1973 he was replaced by V. P. Chuhaiov, formerly ideological secretary of the Lviv oblast party committee.[103] The practice of appointing party functionaries to the leadership of the Institute of History had begun prior to Shelest's fall, notably with A. D. Skaba's appointment in 1968. Skaba was replaced in 1973 by A. H. Sheveliev, a former functionary of the Komsomol in Kiev and secretary of the Kiev city party committee.[104] In 1978 Sheveliev was implicated in a scandal involving the theft and resale of books from the institute's library.[105] The same year he was replaced by the present director, Iu. Iu. Kondufor, formerly head of the Propaganda and Agitation Department in Kharkiv and head of the Science and Culture Department of the Central Committee.[106]

Although Ukrainian historical scholarship continues to be tightly controlled by the party's ideological apparatus, there have been some signs of progress even in this area. Most notably, Ivanchenko (Ivanova), who was severely criticized in *Komunist Ukrainy* for her book *Mykhailo Drahomanov u suspilno-politychnomu rusi Rosii ta Ukrainy (II polovyna XIX st.)* (1971), has resumed her work on the nineteenth century, and in 1977 she was admitted to the Writers' Union. The most recent edition of the handbook of writers in Ukraine lists the aforementioned book on Drahomanov among her major publications.[107] Does this suggest that an attempt is under way to rehabilitate the nineteenth-century Ukrainian political thinker? If so, it would come as a welcome surprise in view of the difficulties that Drahomanov has posed for Soviet historians since the 1920s.[108] In September and October 1981, however, several publications in Kiev marked the 140th anniversary of Drahomanov's birth with short articles, including a controversial piece by Serhii Bilokin in *Literaturna Ukraina*.[109] Another well-known historian who appears to be making a comeback is Olena Kompan, a specialist on Ukrainian cultural history, who was dismissed from her position in the Institute of Archeology during the post-Shelest purge.[110]

In 1978 the Presidium of the Ukrainian Academy of Sciences discussed the work of the Institute of History during the period 1973–7, criticizing the latter's neglect of "such important problems and periods in the history of Ukraine as the development of Kievan Rus', the history of the twelfth to the seventeenth centuries, [and] the history of culture in Ukraine in the prerevolutionary period."[111] I. F. Kuras, head of the Social Sciences Sector of the Science and Educational Institutions Department of the Central Committee, made the same observation at a round table discussion on the development of historical studies in the republic, organized by *Ukrainskyi istorychnyi zhurnal*.[112] Recently there has been a spate of articles and scholarly conferences on the pre-Soviet period in Ukrainian history, which is attributable to the celebrations marking the 1500th anniversary of Kiev. Not to be outdone by the historians, Ukrainian writers have filled the literary journals with works on historical themes that predate Lenin and the Bolsheviks. The quality of these efforts is best left to the judgment of specialists. However, few would argue that the translation and publication of such works as Beauplan's seventeenth century *Description of Ukraine* is not a worthwhile undertaking.[113] In the 1970s, the pre-1917 period was a virtual *terra incognita* for Soviet

Ukrainian historiography. The current emphasis on this period may have a long-term impact quite different from that foreseen by the political overseers of the historian's craft.

Another positive development has been the revival of interest in local history, which is closely tied to the activities of the Ukrainian Society for the Protection of Historical and Cultural Monuments headed by P. T. Tronko. Articles and letters have appeared in the press decrying the state of some of Ukraine's historical antiquities and urging a serious scholarly approach to the study of local history, including the establishment of a specialized journal in the field.[114] In 1979 a Department of Local History Research was formed in the Institute of History, and the following year the first republican conference on local history was convened in Poltava. Thus far a catalogue of all historical and cultural monuments in Ukraine under state protection—the first of its kind in the republic—has been prepared for publication, and a decision has been taken to establish a Republican Scientific Council on Problems of Local History Research in the Institute of History.[115] At the same time, it must be emphasized that national historiography remains a sensitive political issue. Thus, academician Fedoseev has recently restated official concern about "idealization" of the Zaporozhian Sich, while simultaneously cautioning against a one-sided interpretation of the significance of Peter I's reign for the development of the Russian state.[116]

Clearly, the "cultural detente" that we are currently witnessing in Ukraine in no way implies fundamental changes in overall Soviet nationalities policy. The driving force behind that policy remains Moscow's determination to attain the greatest possible degree of ideological, social, economic and cultural unity of its vast multinational population: hence the magic formula of the "Soviet people" and the renewed campaign to raise the Russian language to the status of the "second native language" of the non-Russian nations.[117]

Ukrainians (and Belorussians), by virtue of their historical and linguistic ties to the Russians, have been assigned the role of junior partners to their Eastern neighbour in the formidable task of moulding a Russian-speaking Slavic bloc in the USSR which is to serve as the basis of the Soviet people. This project has assumed particular urgency as the Russians confront the prospect of becoming a minority in the Soviet Union. Ukrainians are encouraged to view themselves, together with the Russians and Belorussians, as having evolved from a "single early Rus' nationality" (*iedyna davnoruska narodnist*) that is said to have had a common state and a common language. The Soviet interpretation of Ukrainian history is that Ukraine and the Ukrainians emerged on the face of the earth for one reason and one reason only: to be "reunited" with Russia and the Russians.[118] Mykola Kotliar, a Soviet specialist on the

Kievan Rus' period, has argued that even after the formation of the Russian, Ukrainian and Belorussian nations, which he dates to the end of the fifteenth century, all three "nonetheless continued to view themselves as a single Rus' people also in the sixteenth and seventeenth centuries." Moreover, says Kotliar, "that is why reunification was so readily and joyfully received in Ukraine and in Russia."[119] The unmistakable suggestion is that national distinctions between Ukrainians and Russians were really not very significant in the past and that this applies to the present and future as well. Another dimension of the quest for Ukrainian-Russian unity involves emphasis on the "blood-related" (*iedynokrovnyi*) link between the two nations, which is to be found in the speeches and articles of Ukrainian party leaders.[120] An enterprising Soviet scholar has even written a monograph on the subject. Its purpose and methodology are described as follows:

> The basis for this research is the study of the serum and red cell systems of the blood. Questions of the genetic affinity of the three East Slavic peoples are elucidated; the racist fabrications of Ukrainian bourgeois nationalists about their glaring genetic differences are refuted; and the current process of the ethnic drawing together of these people are examined.[121]

In recent years the present regime has intensified its efforts to obliterate Ukrainian national consciousness by creating an historical framework for Russo-Ukrainian relations that would enhance the further integration of Ukrainians with their "elder brother." Thus, the main message of the 1979 celebrations of the "reunification" of Ukraine with Russia was the historical inevitability of an eternal unity of the two peoples. Addressing the commemorative meeting held on 30 January in Kiev to mark this event, Shcherbytsky announced that "the Ukrainian and Russian peoples reunited in an indissoluble fraternal union 325 years ago. And today, at this solemn hour, the people of Ukraine declare: that is how it was, how it is, and how it will be forever!"[122] Ukrainians, in effect, are thereby deprived of a separate and distinct identity either in the past, present, or future.[123]

An even more ambitious project now under way is the attempt to portray the contemporary USSR together with its Soviet people and all-Union Russian language as the final product of a progressive linear development that has its origins in the Kievan state and includes the pre-1917 Russian absolute monarchy.[124] At the joint session of the USSR and Ukrainian Academies of Sciences convened on 14 April 1982 to observe the 1500th anniversary of Kiev, academician Fedoseev argued quite unabashedly that the Russian centralized state was the heir to all that was positive in the Kievan Rus' period. "As a result," he maintained, "the significance of the historical legacy of Kievan Rus' is, above all, in its having established the material, social, and cultural preconditions for the formation of the centralized state."[125] The analogy between the Soviet Union and Kievan Rus' is further underscored by allusions to the multinational composition of both states. Although Kievan Rus' is described as the wellspring of the Russians, Ukrainians and Belorussians, Fedoseev notes that "also more than twenty non-Slavic peoples of the Baltic, the North, the Volga region, the Northern Caucasus and the Black Sea region took the first steps in their social and political development within the framework of this state."[126] A similar argument, but from the linguistic standpoint, was made several years ago by F. P. Filin, a corresponding member of the USSR Academy of Sciences and director of its Russian Language Institute. Emphasizing the multinational character of Kievan Rus', Filin argued that

> the Russian language appeared a long time ago. When the early Rus' state emerged, with its centre in Kiev, the early Rus' language existed; it was the direct ancestor of the Russian, Ukrainian, and Belorussian languages, and already then it served not only the one early Rus' people. Early Rus' included other tribes and peoples as well—Finno-Ugric, Turkic, Baltic, Iranian and others—and these tribes gradually adhered to the Russian language.[127]

Are we to understand that the USSR, complete with prototypes of the Soviet people and a "language of inter-nationality discourse and unity," was somehow preordained already at the end of the fifth century?

Whether or not the "Soviet people" will become a reality remains to be seen. Soviet doctrine claims that such a "new historical community of people" has already been established, but that in no way is it tantamount to the formation of a "Soviet nation." This was firmly laid down by Brezhnev in his 4 October 1977 speech on the draft of the new Soviet constitution.[128] Taking their cue from the Soviet party leader, prominent experts on nationalities policy have argued that the emergence of the Soviet people "by no means leads to the disappearance of existing nations and nationalities."[129] Yet, in recent years it has become customary for the Ukrainian party leaders like Shcherbytsky to use the geographical expression "people of Ukraine" (*narod Ukrainy*) when referring to the republic's population, thereby de-emphasizing the ethnic factor. This has been noted in Moscow and infused with specific ideological content.[130] Thus, it is not at all surprising to learn from a Ukrainian Komsomol newspaper that recently a group of young people from Dnipropetrovsk, when asked by students in London where they were from, explained: "From the Soviet Union. That is what Russia has been called for sixty years now."[131] Was this a mere slip of the tongue, or is it perhaps an indication of the direction one is obliged to take along the road to "Soviet peoplehood?"

Notes

1. See, for example, G. Hodnett, "What's in a Nation?," *Problems of Communism* 16, no. 5 (September-October 1967): 3; R. Szporluk, "Nationalities and the Russian Problem in the U.S.S.R.: An Historical Outline," *Journal of International Affairs* 27, no. 1 (1973): 36–7; and T. Rakowska-Harmstone, "The Dialectics of Nationalism in the USSR," *Problems of Communism* 23, no. 3 (May-June 1974): 18–19.

2. T. Rakowska-Harmstone, "The Dilemma of Nationalism in the Soviet Union," in *The Soviet Union under Brezhnev and Kosygin: The Transition Years*, ed. J. W. Strong (New York 1971), 127–8.

3. M. I. Kulichenko, *Natsionalnye otnosheniia v SSSR i tendentsii ikh razvitiia* (Moscow 1972), 404.

4. See, for example, Brezhnev's speech in Alma-Ata on 15 August 1973, in which he asserts that national distinctions are not disappearing and rejects the idea that the merger of nations in the USSR is an accomplished fact. L. I. Brezhnev, *Leninskim kursom. Rechi i stati*, 8 vols. to date (Moscow 1974), 4: 243.

5. I. P. Tsamerian, "Nekotorye aktualnye voprosy teorii natsii i natsionalnykh otnoshenii," *Nauchnyi kommunizm*, no. 2 (1979): 31.

6. *Realnyi sotsializm v SSSR i ego burzhuaznye falsifikatory* (Moscow 1977), 297.

7. P. N. Fedoseev, "Teoreticheskie problemy razvitiia i sblizheniia sotsialisticheskikh natsii," *Vestnik Akademii nauk SSSR*, no. 12 (1979): 35.

8. See, for example, the criticism of one E. P. Menkin for maintaining that "the merger of nations and nationalities is occurring under the conditions of socialism" in K. L. Korneev, "Rastsvet i sblizhenie sotsialisticheskikh natsii i narodnostei," *Nauchnyi kommunizm*, no. 3 (1979): 40.

9. R. F. Vinokurova, "Obsuzhdenie stati P. M. Rogacheva i M. A. Sverdlina 'O poniatii "natsiia" '," *Voprosy istorii*, no. 2 (1966): 169. For an analysis of the discussion, see Hodnett, "What's in a Nation?," 2–15, and "K itogam diskussii po nekotorym problemam teorii natsii," *Voprosy istorii*, no. 8 (1970): 86–98.

10. E. A. Bagramov, *Leninskaia natsionalnaia politika: Dostizheniia i perspektivy* (Moscow 1977), 155. See also V. K. Sulzhenko, "Komunistychne budivnytstvo i rozvytok natsionalnykh vidnosyn," *Komunist Ukrainy*, no. 3 (1972): 70; and I. P. Holovakha, F. Ia. Horovsky and V. A. Chyrko, "Za hlyboke doslidzhennia pytan leninskoi natsionalnoi polityky KPRS," *Komunist Ukrainy*, no. 11 (1972): 88.

11. M. I. Kulichenko, "Razrabotka problemy novoi istoricheskoi obshchnosti v sovetskoi istoriografii," in *Osnovnye napravleniia izucheniia natsionalnykh otnoshenii v SSSR* (Moscow 1979), 38–9.

12. "Torzhestvo leninskoi natsionalnoi politiki," *Kommunist*, no. 13 (1969): 10.

13. *Spravochnik partiinogo rabotnika*, vypusk 10 (Moscow 1970), 40.

14. M. I. Kulichenko, "Obrazovanie i razvitie sovetskogo naroda kak novoi istoricheskoi obshchnosti," *Voprosy istorii*, no. 4 (1979): 7. See also

A. V. Lykholat and N. V. Komarenko, "Osnovni napriamy u vysvitlenni problemy 'Radianskyi narod—nova istorychna spilnist liudei'," *Ukrainskyi istorychnyi zhurnal*, no. 1 (1976): 50. For a recent Western analysis, see Y. Bilinsky, "The Concept of the Soviet People and its Implications for Soviet Nationality Policy," *Annals of the Ukrainian Academy of Sciences in the United States* 14, no. 37–8 (1978–80): 87–133.

15. *Samvydav* is the Ukrainian equivalent of the Russian term *samizdat*, which means self-publishing and refers to unofficial publications. For a survey of the development of Ukrainian dissent, see B. R. Bociurkiw, "Soviet Nationalities Policy and Dissent in the Ukraine," *The World Today* 30, no. 5 (May 1974): 214–26; J. Birch, "The Nature and Sources of Dissidence in Ukraine," in *Ukraine in the Seventies*, ed. P. J. Potichnyj (Oakville, Ont. 1975), 307–30; and K. C. Farmer, *Ukrainian Nationalism in the Post-Stalin Era: Myth, Symbols and Ideology in Soviet Nationalities Policy* (The Hague-Boston-London 1980), 78ff.

16. V. Moroz, "Pochatky i verkhy ukrainskoho samostavannia v 60-ykh i 70-ykh rokakh," *Ukrainski visti* (Detroit), 4 October 1981.

17. See J. Pelenski, "Shelest and His Period in Soviet Ukraine (1963–1972): A Revival of Controlled Ukrainian Autonomism," in *Ukraine in the Seventies*, 283–305.

18. Bociurkiw, "Soviet Nationalities Policy and Dissent," 220.

19. See Pelenski, "Shelest and His Period," and Y. Bilinsky, "Mykola Skrypnyk and Petro Shelest: An Essay on the Persistence and Limits of Ukrainian National Communism," in *Soviet Nationality Policies and Practices*, ed. J. R. Azrael (New York 1978), 105–43.

20. J. Kolasky, *Two Years in Soviet Ukraine* (Toronto 1970), 206.

21. I. I. Groshev, *Borba partii protiv natsionalizma* (Moscow 1974), 111.

22. Ibid., 115.

23. This is the position held by G. Hodnett, "Ukrainian Politics and the Purge of Shelest," paper presented at the Midwest Slavic Conference, Ann Arbor, Michigan, 5–7 May 1977. An excerpt from this paper has recently been published as "The Views of Petro Shelest," *Annals of the Ukrainian Academy of Arts and Sciences in the United States* 14, no. 37–8 (1978–80): 209–43.

24. This view, often accompanied by little or no substantiating data, continues to find its way into the published literature. See, for example, P. J. Murphy, *Brezhnev: Soviet Politician* (Jefferson, N.C. 1981), 288–90.

25. To my knowledge, no Soviet source has ever accused Shelest, directly or indirectly, of "incorrect" views on foreign policy issues. On the contrary, Soviet sources consistently link the Ukrainian party leader with domestic policies. In addition to Groshev, see Iu. E. Volkova, *Istoricheskii opyt borby KPSS protiv natsionalizma* (Moscow 1975), 43, concerning the Ukrainian party's work in "overcoming mistakes of a nationalist character in the ideological life of the country," and the statement in the latest edition of *Narysy istorii Komunistychnoi partii Ukrainy*, 4th ed. (Kiev 1977), 688–9, that Shelest was removed for "serious shortcomings in the leadership of the republican party organization."

26. R. Szporluk, *Ukraine: A Brief History*, 2d ed. (Detroit 1982), 122–3.

27. J. A. Armstrong, "The Ethnic Scene in the Soviet Union: The View of the Dictatorship," in *Ethnic Minorities in the Soviet Union*, ed. E. Goldhagen (New York 1968), 32.

28. " 'To Ensure a Peaceful and Dignified Life'," *Soviet Life*, no. 5, (1982): 10.

29. For an exhaustive analysis, see Hodnett, "Ukrainian Politics and the Purge of Shelest." See also M. Prokop, "Padinnia Petra Shelesta," *Suchasnist* 13, no. 6 (June 1973): 98–110; and Y. Bilinsky, "The Communist Party of Ukraine After 1966," in *Ukraine in the Seventies*, 239–66, and "Politics, Purge, and Dissent in the Ukraine since the Fall of Shelest," in *Nationalism and Human Rights: Processes of Modernization in the USSR*, ed. I. Kamenetsky (Littleton, Colo. 1977), 168–85.

30. See the official biographies in *Deputaty Verkhovnogo Soveta SSSR. Sedmoi sozyv* (Moscow 1966), 319 and 497.

31. Pelenski, "Shelest and His Period," 285.

32. *Sovetskaia kultura*, 4 June 1968. See also the article by N. Fed in *Izvestiia*, 13 June 1968.

33. For details, see *Molod Dnipropetrovska v borotbi proty rusyfikatsii* (Munich 1971).

34. Earlier, on 9 June 1972, O. P. Liashko was released as chairman of the Presidium of the Supreme Soviet and appointed chairman of the Council of Ministers in place of Shcherbytsky, and at the 27 July 1972 plenum of the Central Committee, I. S. Hrushetsky, chairman of the Central Committee's Party Commission, was promoted to full membership in the Politburo. On the following day he was elected chairman of the Presidium of the Supreme Soviet in place of Liashko.

35. Malanchuk's promotion to the Secretariat was accompanied by his election to candidate membership in the Politburo. For a characterization of Malanchuk, see B. Lewićkyj, "Nowy szef ideologiczny w Kijowie," *Kultura*, no. 12/303 (December 1972): 60–2.

36. Hodnett, "Ukrainian Politics and the Purge of Shelest," 67–8.

37. *Komunist Ukrainy*, no. 11 (1972): 96. Terletsky, a Doctor of Historical Sciences, assumed the chief editorship of the journal with the January 1969 issue. In 1967 he became head of a department of the Institute of State and Law of the Ukrainian Academy of Sciences, with which he has been associated since 1958. For an official biography, see *Radianska entsyklopediia istorii Ukrainy*, 4 vols. (Kiev 1972), 4: 263. V. F. Sokurenko, a Candidate of Historical Sciences, had previously been director of the Kiev branch of the Central Museum of V. I. Lenin. See *Radianska Ukraina*, 7 April 1970. There were no further changes in the composition of the editorial board until April 1973.

38. Tsvietkov was removed from the editorial board of *Komunist Ukrainy* in April 1973. Like Terletsky, Tsvietkov's position in the Ukrainian Academy of Sciences, to which he was elected a corresponding member in 1972, was not

affected by the purge. In 1973 he was transferred to head a department of the academy's Institute of State and Law. See *Istoriia Akademii nauk Ukrainskoi SSR* (Kiev 1979), 790–1. Rudych was identified in his new position in March 1973 during the General Assembly of the Academy of Sciences. See *Visnyk Akademii nauk Ukrainskoi RSR*, no. 6 (1973): 33. In April 1973 he joined the editorial board of *Komunist Ukrainy*.

The "sanctity" of membership in the Academy of Sciences applies to Shelest's son, Vitalii, as well. He remains a corresponding member of the Ukrainian Academy of Sciences albeit in Moscow, where from 1974 to 1976 he worked in the Institute of Mathematics of the USSR Academy of Sciences. Since 1976 he has been Deputy Director of the All-Union Research Institute of Physical-Technical and Radio-Technical Measurements in Moscow. See *Istoriia Akademii nauk Ukrainskoi SSR*, 793. In 1978 the Atomizdat publishers in Moscow issued his book *Novyi krug*.

39. *Radianska Ukraina*, 16 October 1973. It remains to be explained why Orel was made a member of the editorial board of *Komunist Ukrainy* in April 1973 only to be dismissed as "agitprop" chief seven months later and then dropped from the editorial board in January 1974. Currently, he holds the position of first deputy chairman of the "Znannia" Society of the Ukrainian SSR. See *Komsomolskoe znamia*, 14 February 1982.

40. Ishchenko was identified in his new position in *Radianska Ukraina*, 18 October 1973. In January 1974 Fedchenko was dropped from the editorial board of *Komunist Ukrainy*.

41. The *samvydav* journal *Ukrainskyi visnyk*, no. 7–8 (Spring 1974) (Paris-Baltimore-Toronto 1975), 116, incorrectly renders Chekaniuk as "Chekaliuk." Chekaniuk also remains a corresponding member of the Academy of Sciences in Kiev. In 1973 he was awarded the title of professor. See *Istoriia Akademii nauk Ukrainskoi SSR*, 791.

42. Ibid., 795.

43. *Literaturna Ukraina*, 27 March 1973.

44. *Radianska Ukraina*, 14 November 1973. On Dadenkov's support for Ukrainianization of the republic's institutions of higher education, see V. Chornovil, "Iak i shcho obstoiuie Bohdan Stenchuk," in *Ukrainskyi visnyk*, no. 6 (March 1972) (Paris-Baltimore 1972), 15ff., and *Ukrainskyi visnyk*, no. 7–8, 121.

45. On 26 December 1975 Degtiarev was appointed chairman of the Ukrainian SSR State Committee for the Supervision of Safe Work Practices in Industry and Mine Supervision, and on 6 January 1976 he was dismissed as first secretary of the Donetsk party organization. See *Radianska Ukraina*, 27 December 1975 and 7 January 1976, and *XXV zizd Komunistychnoi partii Ukrainy 10–13 liutoho 1976 roku. Stenohrafichnyi zvit* (Kiev 1976), 62.

46. *Radianska Ukraina*, 11 January 1976; *Ukrainskyi visnyk*, no. 7–8, 114.

47. M. Prokop, "Ukraina pislia Shelesta i samvydavu," *Suchasnist* 13, no. 7–8 (July-August 1973): 180; and R. Kupchynsky's introduction to *Pohrom v Ukraini 1972–1979* (Munich 1981), 20.

48. See *Istoriia Akademii nauk Ukrainskoi SSR*, 740–1, and "50-richchia akademika V. I. Shynkaruka," *Visnyk Akademii nauk Ukrainskoi RSR*, no. 5 (1978): 105.
49. Hodnett, "Ukrainian Politics and the Purge of Shelest," 64.
50. *Radianska Ukraina*, 29 November 1973.
51. *Ukrainskyi visnyk*, no. 7–8, 113.
52. On 7 April 1970, Ulanov's predecessor, V. M. Tsybulko, was elected first secretary of the Kiev oblast party committee, and on 14 August 1970 a plenum of the Dnipropetrovsk city party committee released Ulanov from his position as first secretary "in connection with his transfer to other work." See *Radianska Ukraina*, 8 April 1970, and *Pravda Ukrainy*, 15 August 1970.
53. For Ulanov's transfer to Voroshylovhrad, see *Radianska Ukraina*, 26 July 1972.
54. Hodnett, "Ukrainian Politics and the Purge of Shelest," 64–8.
55. *Ukrainskyi visnyk*, no. 7–8, 118. This source also states (page 116) that 25 per cent of all ideological secretaries on the oblast, city, and raion party committee levels were purged.
56. Bilinsky, "Politics, Purge, and Dissent in the Ukraine since the Fall of Shelest," 173–4.
57. *Narysy istorii Komunistychnoi partii Ukrainy*, 706. See also *Komunistychna partiia Ukrainy—boiovyi zahin KPRS* (Kiev 1976), 17.
58. The ideological offensive in scholarship, literature and the arts after Shelest's ouster is a broad topic that deserves a separate study and cannot be adequately treated here. In addition to the works already cited, see G. S. N. Luckyj, "The Ukrainian Literary Scene Today," *Slavic Review* 31, no. 4 (December 1972): 863–9; B. Kravtsiv, "Pid praporom pohromnytstva," *Suchasnist* 13, no. 5 (May 1973): 35–50; I. Koshelivets, "Do suchasnoi literaturnoi sytuatsii na Ukraini," *Suchasnist* 13, no. 7–8 (July-August 1973): 97–111; I. Koshelivets, "Shche do literaturnoi sytuatsii na Ukraini," *Suchasnist* 13, no. 9 (September 1973): 28–38; M. Prokop, "Nastup na druhyi front samooborony narodu," *Suchasnist* 13, no. 9 (September 1973): 93–105; R. Kupchynsky, "Pro 'idealizatsiiu, partiinist i patriiarkhalshchynu'," *Suchasnist* 13, no. 11 (November 1973): 75–86; R. Szporluk, "The Ukraine and the Ukrainians," in *Handbook of Major Soviet Nationalities*, ed. Z. Katz (New York 1975), 27ff.; and L. Tillett, "Ukrainian Nationalism and the Fall of Shelest," *Slavic Review* 34, no. 4 (December 1975): 752–68.
59. "Pro seriozni nedoliky ta pomylky odniiei knyhy," *Komunist Ukrainy*, no. 4 (1973): 77–82. See also *Za shcho usunuly Shelesta? Dokumenty* (Munich 1973).
60. Prokop, "Ukraina pislia Shelesta i samvydavu," 179.
61. *Radianska Ukraina*, 27 April 1979. Malanchuk was succeeded by O. S. Kapto, a graduate of Dnipropetrovsk State University and former first secretary of the Ukrainian Komsomol. He was head of the Culture Department from (at least) April 1978.

62. *O dalneishem uluchshenii ideologicheskoi, politiko-vospitatelnoi raboty. Postanovlenie TsK KPSS ot 26 aprelia 1979 goda* (Moscow 1979). A summary of the decree was first published in *Pravda*, 6 May 1979.

63. *Radianska Ukraina*, 8 June 1979.

64. Ibid., 13 February 1981.

65. Ibid., 28 June 1979.

66. E. A. Bagramov, "XXVI sezd KPSS i razvitie natsionalnykh otnoshenii v SSSR," *Voprosy istorii KPSS*, no. 11 (1981): 149; M. N. Guboglo, "V Nauchnom sovete po natsionalnym problemam," *Istoriia SSSR*, no. 4 (1982): 208.

67. *Radianska Ukraina*, 4 July 1979.

68. Ibid., 8 June 1979.

69. See R. Solchanyk, "Ukraine's Ideology Chief Purged," *Soviet Analyst* 8, no. 17 (30 August 1979): 2–4.

70. On the Ukrainian Helsinki Group, see *The Human Rights Movement in Ukraine: Documents of the Ukrainian Helsinki Group 1976–1980*, ed. L. Verba and B. Yasen (Baltimore-Washington-Toronto 1980); Y. Bilinsky and T. Parming, "Helsinki Watch Committees in the Soviet Republics: Implications for Soviet Nationality Policy," *Nationalities Papers* 9, no. 1 (Spring 1981): 1–25; and Bohdan Nahaylo's contribution to the present volume.

71. See, respectively, *Literaturna Ukraina*, 10 January and 28 August 1977; *Literaturna Ukraina*, 13 May 1977; *Literaturna Ukraina*, 19 July 1977; *Molod Ukrainy*, 14 September 1977; *Kultura i zhyttia*, 13 October 1977; *Kultura i zhyttia*, 12 February 1978. See also the commentary by Vitalii Vynohradsky, former chief editor of *Literaturna Ukraina*, in the 21 October 1977 issue of the newspaper.

72. See *Visti z Ukrainy*, 20 April 1972, and M. Iu. Braichevsky, "'Ruska Pravda' pro vtechi vid feodalnoho hnitu," *Ukrainskyi istorychnyi zhurnal*, no. 11 (1977): 104–8.

73. See Ia. E. Borovsky, *Pokhodzhennia Kyieva. Istoriohrafichnyi narys* (Kiev 1980), 116–20ff.

74. Kochur's articles and translations have recently appeared in *Literaturna Ukraina*, 13 March 1981; *Vsesvit*, no. 12 (1980): 162–6; and *Vsesvit*, no. 6 (1981): 183–6. See also *Zhovten*, no. 4 (1981): 140, regarding his participation in the translation of Pierre-Jean Béranger's songs into Ukrainian. For Pavlychko's report, see *Literaturna Ukraina*, 17 April 1981.

75. *Pysmennyky Radianskoi Ukrainy. Biobibliohrafichnyi dovidnyk* (Kiev 1981).

76. "U Viddilenni literatury, movy ta mystetstvoznavstva AN URSR," *Radianske literaturoznavstvo*, no. 6 (1978): 95; and *Istoriia Akademii nauk Ukrainskoi SSR*, 740.

77. *Literaturna Ukraina*, 12 January 1979.

78. Ibid., 26 December 1980.

79. Ibid., 14 and 18 March 1980. Perebyinis has since requested to be relieved of

his position. His replacement is Borys Rohoza, formerly director of the Radianskyi pysmennyk publishing house. See *Literaturna Ukraina*, 17 November 1981.

80. Vynohradsky's election to membership in the Ukrainian Writers' Union was announced in *Literaturna Ukraina*, 5 December 1975.
81. *Radianska Ukraina*, 26 July 1980; *Literaturna Ukraina*, 29 July 1980.
82. *Literaturna Ukraina*, 24 April 1981.
83. Ibid., 21 April 1981.
84. *Novi knyhy Ukrainy. Kataloh vydan ukrainskoiu movoiu No. 1a 1972 roku* (Moscow 1971): 214–15. See "Vytiaz molodoi ukrainskoi poezii," *Visti z Ukrainy*, 4 June 1981, and V. Morenets, "Vasyl Symonenko: Filosofiia pochuttia," *Vitchyzna*, no. 11 (1981): 173–81.
85. *Radianska Ukraina*, 14 December 1980.
86. The publication of an annual almanac entitled *Ukrainskaia literatura segodnia*, which was announced by Radio Kiev, in English, on 9 August 1981, and the establishment of the Ivan Franko Literary Prize for the best foreign translations and popularization of Ukrainian literature are direct responses to complaints voiced at the most recent writers' congress about the anonymity of Ukrainian writers outside the USSR. See *Literaturna Ukraina*, 4 September 1981.
87. *Radianska Ukraina*, 12 February 1981.
88. Ibid., 5 November 1981. For details, see R. Solchanyk, "Shcherbitsky and the Ukrainian Cultural Intelligentsia Meet 'to Exchange Ideas'," *Radio Liberty Research* 455/81, 13 November 1981.
89. See Malanchuk's article "Nauchnost, ideinaia stoikost, klassovoi podkhod," in *Pravda Ukrainy*, 29 June 1971, and his "Dvi kontseptsii mynuloho i suchasnoho Ukrainy," *Zhovten*, no. 1 (1972): 101–9; no. 3, 97–107; no. 4, 96–108; and no. 5, 110–21. At a plenum of the Lviv oblast party committee held on 20 November 1971, local scholars and university lecturers were accused of "praising, whitewashing, and embellishing certain ideologues of Ukrainian bourgeois nationalism" in their treatment of the historical past. See *Pravda*, 1 December 1971.
90. Pelenski, "Shelest and His Period," 288; *Ukrainskyi visnyk*, no. 7–8, 127–8.
91. I. V. Khmil, "Zahalni zbory Viddilennia ekonomiky, istorii, filosofii ta prava Akademii nauk Ukrainskoi RSR," *Ukrainskyi istorychnyi zhurnal*, no. 5 (1973): 149.
92. *Radianska Ukraina*, 17 March 1973.
93. Ibid., 20 April 1973.
94. V. Iu. Malanchuk, "Ideini dzherela literatury," *Vitchyzna*, no. 12 (1973): 11–13.
95. *Radianska Ukraina*, 17 May 1974.
96. V. Shcherbytsky, *Vospityvat soznatelnykh, aktivnykh stroitelei kommunizma* (Moscow 1974), 13; I. F. Kuras, "Aktualni zavdannia istorychnoi nauky (Respublikanska narada uchenykh-istorykiv)," *Komunist Ukrainy*, no. 1 (1975): 75.

97. For a stinging indictment of the party's policies in this area, see Iu. Badzio's *Vidkrytyi lyst do Prezydii Verkhovnoi Rady Soiuzu RSR ta Tsentralnoho Komitetu KPRS* (New York 1980), 47ff.

98. This information is based on the annual publications *Novi knyhy Ukrainy* (Moscow) and *Knyhy vydavnytstv Ukrainy* (Kharkiv). See also Pelenski, "Shelest And His Period," 287; F. Sysyn's review of the first issue of *Seredni viky na Ukraini* in *Recenzija* 2, no. 2 (Spring 1972): 87–93; O. Pritsak, "A Serial Publication and a Political Era: An Obituary with a Post Scriptum," *Recenzija* 6, no. 2 (Spring-Summer 1976): 31–51; and I. Hvat, "Ukraina v 70-kh rokakh (Pro odyn z naslidkiv pohromu inteligentsii ta padinnia Shelesta)," *Ukrainske slovo* (Paris), 28 March 1982.

99. On the planned publication of this source, which was being prepared jointly by the Institute of History and the Central State Historical Archive of the Ukrainian SSR, see "Litopys Zaporozkoi Sichi," *Visti z Ukrainy*, no. 8 (February 1968) and the short note in *Vitchyzna*, no. 5 (1968): 220.

100. "Sesiia Zahalnykh zboriv Akademii nauk Ukrainskoi RSR," *Visnyk Akademii nauk Ukrainskoi RSR*, no. 6 (1973): 23.

101. Ibid., 31. Judging from Rostyslav Bratun's address to the Seventh Congress of the Writers' Union of Ukraine in April 1976, more than one department in the institute was closed in the process of its reorganization. See *VII zizd pysmennykiv Radianskoi Ukrainy 14–16 kvitnia 1976 roku. Materialy zizdu* (Kiev 1977), 88.

102. "Sesiia Zahalnykh zboriv Akademii nauk Ukrainskoi SSR," 31.

103. *Istoriia Akademii nauk Ukrainskoi SSR*, 662. In January 1972 Oleksiuk was criticized in *Komunist Ukrainy* for his attempt to rehabilitate the Western Ukrainian socialist Volodymyr Levynsky. He subsequently "corrected" his views, but was nonetheless ousted from the directorship of the institute. See O. Ia. Lysenko, V. I. Soldatov and A. I. Uiomov, "Pidvyshchuvaty riven filosofskykh doslidzhen. Po storinkakh zhurnalu 'Filosofska dumka'," *Komunist Ukrainy*, no. 1 (1972): 94, and Myroslav Oleksiuk, "Levynsky bez masky," *Zhovten*, no. 4 (1972): 109–12.

104. *Istoriia Akademii nauk Ukrainskoi SSR*, 792.

105. For details, see R. Solchanyk, "Case No. 2–71 and the Fall of Arnold Shevelyev," *Radio Liberty Research* 84/79, 13 March 1979.

106. *Ucheni vuziv Ukrainskoi RSR* (Kiev 1968), 219.

107. *Pysmennyky Radianskoi Ukrainy*, 97. For the attack on Ivanchenko (Ivanova), see M. I. Suprunenko, "Krytychni zauvazhennia do monohrafii pro M. P. Drahomanova," *Komunist Ukrainy*, no. 11 (1972): 93–5.

108. In addition to the criticism of Ivanchenko (Ivanova), Drahomanov has figured in the post-Shelest attacks on the works of, among others, V. H. Sarbei and V. S. Dmytrychenko. See M. N. Leshchenko, "Neukhylno dotrymuvatysia leninskoi metodolohii v istorychnomu doslidzhenni," *Komunist Ukrainy*, no. 1 (1974): 88–92, and V. S. Horsky, I. V. Ivano and P. T. Manzenko, "Seriozni khyby v doslidzhenni vazhlyvoi temy," *Filosofska dumka*, no. 6 (1974): 114–18. For a thorough analysis, see Zh. P. Kh. [John-Paul Himka], "Drahomanivska spadshchyna siohodni," *Suchasnist* 14, no. 6 (June (1974): 83–90.

109. "Kalendar zhurnalu Ukraina," *Ukraina*, no. 36 (6 September 1981): 25; I. Khorunzhy, "Naputnyk nepobornoi Lesi," *Ukraina*, no. 38 (20 September 1981): 14–15; M. Yatsenko, "Champion of Social Progress," *News from Ukraine*, no. 43 (October 1981); and S. Bilokin, "Shliakhy do istyny. Pro deiaki aspekty etychnykh zasad M. P. Drahomanova," *Literaturna Ukraina*, 16 October 1981.

110. See her "Pid opikoiu Klio," *Vitchyzna*, no. 6 (1981): 171–8, and her review of Zahrebelny's historical novel *Roksolana* (Kiev 1980) in *Literaturna Ukraina*, 30 October 1981.

111. "Pro diialnist Instytutu istorii," *Visnyk Akademii nauk Ukrainskoi RSR*, no. 5 (1978): 5.

112. " 'Kruhlyi stil' v redaktsii 'Ukrainskoho istorychnoho zhurnalu'," *Ukrainskyi istorychnyi zhurnal*, no. 1 (1981): 11.

113. Beauplan's travelogue, with an introduction by Iaroslav Isaievych, was published in *Zhovten*, no. 4 (1981): 52–88. Isaievych has also translated the early seventeenth-century reminiscences of Kiev and Lviv written by Martin Gruneweg, a German merchant who for a time lived in Lviv. See *Zhovten*, no. 10 (1980): 105–14, and *Vsesvit*, no. 5 (1981): 204–11.

114. See, for example, the letter of seven writers—among them Valerii Shevchuk and Borys Kharchuk—to the editors of *Literaturna Ukraina*, 16 September 1980; I. Barvinok, "Khto vin, kraieznavets?," *Kultura i zhyttia*, 6 September 1981; and F. Bloka, "Sylni, ale roziednani," *Kultura i zhyttia*, 21 February 1982.

115. Iu. Z. Danyliuk, "Respublikanska naukova konferentsiia z istorii kraieznavstva," *Ukrainskyi istorychnyi zhurnal*, no. 1 (1981): 156–7; P. T. Tronko, "Istoricheskoe kraevedenie v Ukrainskoi SSR," *Istoriia SSSR*, no. 1 (1982): 205–8; and P. Tronko, "Na radist suchasnym i pryideshnim pokolinniam," *Literaturna Ukraina*, 11 February 1982.

116. Fedoseev, "Teoreticheskie problemy," 41. See also the interesting remarks by Kulichenko on the book *Az i Ia (Kniga blagonamerennogo chitatelia)* (1975) by the Kazakh writer O. Suleimenov in *Vzaimootnoshenie razvitiia natsionalnykh iazykov i natsionalnykh kultur* (Moscow 1980), 298–9

117. On recent developments in Soviet language policy, see Y. Bilinsky, "Expanding the Use of Russian or Russification?," *Russian Review* 40, no. 3 (July 1981): 317–32, and R. Solchanyk, "Russian Language and Soviet Politics," *Soviet Studies* 34, no. 1 (January 1982): 23–42.

118. See S. M. Horak, "Soviet Historiography and the New Nationalities' Policy, a Case Study: Belorussia and Ukraine," in *Change and Adaptation in Soviet and East European Politics*, ed. J. P. Shapiro and P. J. Potichnyj (New York 1976), 201–16.

119. M. Kotliar, " 'Shchob esmy naviky vsi iedyno buly!'," *Vsesvit*, no. 4 (1979): 189.

120. See, for example, Shcherbytsky's 30 January 1979 speech in Kiev marking the 325th anniversary of the Pereiaslav Treaty in *Radianska Ukraina*, 31 January 1979, and Malanchuk's article "Rastsvet dukhovnoi kultury

ukrainskogo naroda v bratskoi seme narodov SSSR," *Voprosy filosofii*, no. 1 (1979): 4, on the same occasion.

121. R. A. Starovoitova, *Etnicheskaia genogeografiia Ukrainskoi SSR (Gematologicheskoe issledovanie)* (Kiev 1979), 2.

122. *Radianska Ukraina*, 31 January 1979. See also Shcherbytsky's article "Velikaia sila bratskogo edineniia," *Kommunist*, no. 1 (1979): 24–36. For an interesting Chinese commentary on the anniversary celebrations, see "How New Tsars Inherit Their Predecessors' Mantle," *Beijing Review*, no. 17 (27 April 1979): 13–14.

123. The politics of Soviet historiography vis-à-vis Ukrainians is examined in detail by Badzio, *Vidkrytyi lyst do Prezydii*. See also "Vidkrytyi lyst Iuriia Badzia do rosiiskykh ta ukrainskykh istorykiv," *Suchasnist* 20, no. 12 (December 1980): 128–54.

124. Earlier attempts to seek the "historical roots" of the Soviet people have been subjected to criticism in Soviet publications. See I. P. Tsamerian, "Iednist internatsionalnoho i natsionalnoho v novii istorychnii spilnosti—radianskomu narodi," *Filosofska dumka*, no. 6 (1977): 13, and Kulichenko, "Razrabotka problemy novoi istoricheskoi obshchnosti v sovetskoi istoriografii," 53–4.

125. *Radianska Ukraina*, 15 April 1982.

126. Ibid.

127. Radio Moscow, in Russian, 24 January 1979. This was the first programme in a new series of the all-Union radio entitled "Besedy o russkom iazyke." For details, see Z. Liustrova, "Besedy o russkom iazyke," *Govorit i pokazyvaet Moskva*, 1 January 1979.

128. L. I. Brezhnev, *O konstitutsii SSSR. Doklady i vystupleniia* (Moscow 1977), 39–44.

129. P. Fedoseev, "Novaia sotsialnaia i internatsionalnaia obshchnost," *Pravda*, 19 April 1982.

130. G. T. Tavadov, "XXVI sezd KPSS o razvitii natsionalnykh otnoshenii v SSSR," *Nauchnyi kommunizm*, no. 5 (1981): 16.

131. *Molod Ukrainy*, 3 February 1982.

Ukrainian Dissent and Opposition After Shelest

Bohdan Nahaylo

The post-Shelest period has witnessed the persistence and development of Ukrainian dissent.[1] Although dealt a devastating blow by the numerous arrests and trials which accompanied the extensive political and cultural purge in Ukraine in 1972–3, within a relatively short space of time, this phenomenon re-emerged as an embarrassing irritant for the Soviet authorities. The new phase saw the transformation of Ukrainian dissent into a full-fledged human and national rights movement and the crystallization of Ukrainian dissenting thought. Despite the continuous assaults against it by the authorities and the immense difficulties and setbacks which this has caused it, Ukrainian dissent in recent years has demonstrated an extraordinary endemicity and an irrepressible vitality.

This paper examines Ukrainian dissent and opposition in the first five years after Shelest's ouster—a period not only of destruction, but also of germination. It begins with the launching of the KGB offensive against Ukrainian dissent in January 1972 and ends with the arrest in early 1977 of Mykola Rudenko, the leader of the Ukrainian Helsinki monitoring group. Because of limitations of space, this account does not deal with the other main forms of dissidence which exist in Ukraine, that is religious dissent and the Crimean Tatar and Jewish emigration movements.

The 1972 crackdown on Ukrainian dissent, while part of a general drive by the authorities against dissenters throughout the Soviet Union, was exceptional for two reasons. First, its scale and severity made it the "heaviest single KGB assault"[2] sustained by any dissenting group in the USSR in the post-Stalin period. An examination of the available *samvydav* material by the author has revealed the names of 70 Ukrainian dissenters arrested or tried in the two year period 1972–3, though the real figure is reported to have been much higher.[3] Second, the repressive measures against Ukrainian dissenters signalled something far more ambitious and sinister than just a police action aimed at suppressing a group of "malcontents." They were part and parcel of a major purge in Ukraine—subsequently labelled the "General Pogrom" by the *samvydav* journal the *Ukrainian Herald* ("Ukrainskyi visnyk"), no. 7–8[4]—which affected many sectors of Ukrainian society, including the leadership of the Communist Party of Ukraine (CPU), and most notably its first secretary, Petro Shelest.

Though the extent of the "General Pogrom" has yet to be fully assessed, the evidence suggests that the aim of this campaign was to terminate and, if possible, to reverse those social processes which had brought about the revival of cultural and public life in Ukraine during the 1960s. By the end of that decade, the Soviet leadership became concerned about the resurgent national assertiveness of Ukrainians. This development was at variance with an official nationalities policy designed to achieve the "drawing-together" of the many peoples of the USSR into a multinational community—the so-called "Soviet People" (*sovietskii narod*)—in which, despite the internationalist rhetoric, the Russian language and culture would predominate. Two factors were particularly disturbing. The counter-productive arrests and trials of patriotically minded Ukrainian intellectuals in 1965–6 had precipitated the emergence of open dissent and protest, producing such a scathing indictment of the official nationalities policy as Ivan Dziuba's *Internationalism or Russification?*. Shelest's "Ukrainian faction," moreover, was attempting to maintain a *modus vivendi* with the nationally minded Ukrainian intelligentsia. It not only tolerated and, in certain respects, actually promoted a Soviet Ukrainian patriotism, but also sought to co-opt some of the more amenable dissenters into the Soviet Ukrainian "establishment."[5]

At the beginning of the 1970s, it was clear that Shelest's carrot and stick approach to Ukrainian dissent was not working. Dissent was on the increase and its participants were becoming more enterprising. In 1969 Ukrainian dissenters established links with human rights campaigners in Moscow and thereby obtained access to the *samvydav* journal, *A Chronicle of Current Events*. Not long afterward, in January 1970, they started to publish their own journal, the *Ukrainian Herald*.[6] Within a year, four issues had appeared and the important new mouthpiece for Ukrainian dissent seemed established. In July 1970, the long-standing head of the KGB in Ukraine and colleague of Shelest, Vitalii Nikitchenko, was abruptly replaced by Vitalii Fedorchuk, a sign of Moscow's displeasure at events in Ukraine. Several months later, as a warning to others, the historian and former political prisoner, Valentyn Moroz, was given the unusually severe sentence of nine years imprisonment and five years internal exile for writing his powerful protest essays. Instead of discouraging

Ukrainian dissenters, the harsh treatment meted out to Moroz only incensed them and provoked widespread protests. The following year when another well-known Ukrainian dissenter, Nina Strokata, was arrested in Odessa, a group of colleagues, together with the leading Russian human rights campaigner, Piotr Yakir, organized a "Citizens Committee" for her defence, one of the first organizations of this type to be founded in the USSR.[7]

The increasing confidence and self-assertiveness of Ukrainian dissenters was also evident from the *Ukrainian Herald*'s attitude toward Russian dissenting groups. Ukrainian dissent had its own distinctive profile in which the struggle for civil rights was simultaneously a struggle for national rights. The editors of the *Ukrainian Herald* made it quite clear that Ukrainian dissenters did not want their activities to be misrepresented as a campaign simply for "freedom of speech and belief." Moreover, they insisted that co-operation with Russian human rights activists be dependent on the latter's unequivocal recognition of the national rights of the non-Russian nations. Issue no. 3 of the *Ukrainian Herald* (dated October 1970), for instance, dissociated "Ukrainian democratic circles" from the "Programme of the Democrats of Russia, Ukraine and the Baltic."[8] Issue no. 5 criticized the Moscow-based Committee for Human Rights, founded by Dr. Andrei Sakharov, Andrei Tverdokhlebov and Valeri Chalidze, and the Initiative Group for the Defence of Human Rights in the USSR, for not defining their position on the nationalities question. The *Chronicle of Current Events* was praised for the "objectivity, volume and relative accuracy of the information" it supplied, but at the same time it was pointed out that this journal conveyed "an inaccurate idea of the situation in the USSR" because of its concentration on events in Russia, "principally in Moscow." Moreover, the editors of the *Ukrainian Herald* also mentioned the objections of some Ukrainian dissenters who, while not denying the importance of the *Chronicle*, objected to the fact "that it arbitrarily lays claim to some sort of supra-national or all-union character."[9]

It was against this background that the Soviet leadership decided to resort to drastic measures in Ukraine. In order to ensure success, however, it was necessary not only to suppress Ukrainian dissenters and nationally-minded elements of the intelligentsia, but also to sweep aside officials who could be suspected of having fostered in some way the development of a Soviet Ukrainian patriotism. Hence, the magnitude and severity of the "General Pogrom."

According to one account that appeared in *samvydav*, the wave of arrests and searches which began on 12 January 1972 came as a "bolt from the blue."[10] It was not until a month later, after some 20 Ukrainian dissenters had been detained, that authorities made their first attempt to provide an explanation. On 11 February the newspapers *Radianska Ukraina, Pravda Ukrainy* and *Vechirnyi Kiev* announced that in connection with the arrest of a young Ukrainian from Belgium, Iaroslav Dobosh, criminal proceedings had been initiated against Ivan Svitlychny, Viacheslav Chornovil, Ievhen Sverstiuk and others "for conducting activities hostile to the socialist order." Further evidence that the authorities intended to use the "Dobosh affair" to link Ukrainian dissenters with a "foreign anti-Soviet centre"—the "Banderite Organization of Ukrainian Nationalists" (OUN-b)—appeared on 2 March in *Radianska Ukraina* in the form of a letter of recantation from one of the arrested, Zinoviia Franko, granddaughter of the famous Ukrainian poet, Ivan Franko.

In Ukrainian patriotic circles the arrests were immediately interpreted as an anti-Ukrainian action and the official explanation dismissed as a fabricated pretext. Among the first reactions to the crackdown was the circulation in February in *samvydav* of an open letter from a former KGB informer, Boris Kovhar, in which the author revealed in considerable detail how over the years the KGB had been collecting "incriminating" evidence about Ukrainian cultural activists.[11] In March, issue no. 6 of the *Ukrainian Herald* provided details about the arrests and searches, commenting that the KGB was using the "Dobosh affair" "as a pretext to settle accounts with those individuals whom they consider to be the most active in public life."[12]

As was to be expected, protests followed. In May, for example, "A Group of Citizens" from Ukraine sent copies of a protest letter to the Human Rights Committee in Moscow, the Supreme Soviet of the USSR and to the editors of *Izvestiia* and *Literaturna Ukraina* in which they warned that:

> The suppression of national consciousness, the numerous arrests of prominent representatives of the Ukrainian intelligentsia, the threats, blackmail, persecutions and ceaseless mass searches—all this is a threatening reminder that 1937 began in 1933, began with the repression of leading figures of national culture.[13]

On 22 May—the date on which Ukrainian patriotic youth, in accordance with a new tradition begun in the 1960s, commemorated in their own, unofficial manner, the Ukrainian national poet, Taras Shevchenko—a surprisingly large number of people, considering the repressive atmosphere, defiantly braved official displeasure by attempting to gather at the Shevchenko monument in Kiev. As many as 150 persons were reportedly detained and, in some cases, imprisoned for up to fifteen days.[14]

The most substantial and forceful protest document to emerge during this period was the "Open Letter to Members of the Central Committee of the Communist Party of the Soviet Union," written at the beginning of July by two philosophers on the staff of the Institute of Philosophy of the Academy of Sciences of the Ukrainian SSR, Vasyl Lisovy and Ievhen Proniuk.[15] The authors condemned the widespread arrests, searches and interrogations as violations of Soviet constitutional and legal norms. They urged the authorities to ensure that the general public be acquainted with the ideas and writings of the defendants so as to be able to judge for itself whether or not they were guilty of criminal "anti-Soviet" actions. Lisovy and Proniuk were convinced that the KGB offensive in Ukraine was really aimed at suppressing *samvydav* activity. They maintained that the emergence of *samvydav* was a response to the many problems confronting Soviet society and substantiated this argument with a succinct but comprehensive critique of Soviet life.

Echoing Dziuba's argument that the official nationalities policy was not being implemented in accordance with Leninist principles but instead was aimed at the "forced levelling of ethnic characteristics," Lisovy and Proniuk highlighted the acute nature of the nationalities question in Ukraine. The authors detected "a Bacchanalia of Ukrainophobic forces" in the latest wave of repressions, since the victims included not only well-known members of the Ukrainian intelligentsia, but almost all those responsible "for the difficult task of awakening our civic consciousness and national dignity."[16]

As the "General Pogrom" gathered momentum, Shelest and his supporters seemed powerless to intervene. On 18 April, shortly after being expelled from the Writer's Union of Ukraine (WUU), the literary critic and leading Ukrainian dissenter Ivan Dziuba, who ostensibly enjoyed the toleration and protection of the Shelest faction in the CPU, was arrested.[17] In early May, according to a report in *A Chronicle of Current Events* no. 25, "one of Shelest's deputies" received the science fiction writer, Oles Berdnyk, who, in connection with events in Ukraine, had protested that "the KGB had again broken away from the control of the party." The official, confirming Berdnyk's fears, reportedly told him that the leadership of the CPU "was unable to intervene in KGB matters."[18] Several days later, the CPU leader, Petro Shelest, was himself suddenly removed from his post and transferred for work in Moscow as a deputy prime minister of the USSR. The significance of this development may not have been immediately apparent, however, for it was not until April 1973 that he was publicly criticized for his alleged shortcomings in the area of nationalities policy.[19]

As the number of arrests and searches increased, the authorities staged a special press conference in Kiev on 5 June at which Dobosh "confessed" to a "heinous crime against the Soviet state." He admitted working for an "anti-Soviet" nationalist organization in the West and that he had attempted to smuggle *samvydav* out of the USSR. Moreover, he implicated several Ukrainian dissenters.[20] Although Dobosh retracted his "confession" one week later, after being deported from the Soviet Union, the authorities continued their campaign to discredit those arrested. They achieved some success in early July when two of the dissenters being held in custody, the engineer Leonid Selezenko and the poet Mykola Kholodny, publicly recanted in the press and denounced several of their colleagues.[21]

It was only in the summer and autumn of 1972, when many of those arrested were brought to trial and given extremely severe sentences, that it became apparent to what lengths the authorities were prepared to go in order to crush Ukrainian dissent. The first trial in the June series, that of the art teacher, Oleksander Serhiienko, was a travesty of justice and indicated what was to come. The main accusation against Serhiienko was that he had edited parts of Dziuba's *Internationalism or Russification?*. Although he insisted that his alleged editorial corrections were simply notes for his own personal use, he was convicted of "anti-Soviet agitation and propaganda" and sentenced to seven years in a strict-regime labour camp and three years internal exile.[22] Over the next six months, the following Ukrainian dissenters were tried and sentenced to between five and fifteen years imprisonment and internal exile: Zinovii Antoniuk (7 years imprisonment and 3 years internal exile), Vasyl Stus (5 and 3), Ivan Kovalenko (5 imprisonment), Volodymyr Raketsky (5 imprisonment), Iurii Shukhevych (10 and 5), Ivan Hel (10 and 5), Mykhaylo Osadchy (7 and 3), Stefania Shabatura (5 and 3), Iryna Stasiv-Kalynets (6 and 3), Ihor Kalynets (6 and 3), Father Vasyl Romaniuk (7 and 3) and Danylo Shumuk (10 and 5). Boris Kovhar, Mykola Plakhotniuk and subsequently Leonid Pliushch and Vasyl Ruban, were ruled to be mentally ill and confined indefinitely in special psychiatric hospitals for the "especially dangerous." The trials took place against a background of large-scale extra-judicial persecutions of nationally-minded intellectuals, which in many cases resulted in their dismissal. In mid-September, for example, the Presidium of the Academy of Sciences of the Ukrainian SSR, announced a four per cent staff reduction in the various institutions of the academy. Consequently, a large number of leading Ukrainian scholars, including several directors of scholarly institutes, were removed from their posts.[23]

The same pattern continued in 1973. During a purge in the spring at Lviv University, for instance, at least 23 students and 20 professors were dismissed.[24] The trials of dissenters continued. Among those given heavy sentences were Ivan Svitlychny (7 years imprisonment and 5 years internal exile), Ievhen Sverstiuk (7 and 5), Viacheslav Chornovil (6 and 3), Vasyl Lisovy (7 and 3), Ievhen Proniuk (7 and 5) and Valerii Marchenko (6 and 2). Toward the end of the year, the authorities scored a major success by obtaining a public recantation from one of the best known figures in

Ukrainian dissent, Ivan Dziuba, who, after condemning his previous views and activities in a statement published on 9 November in *Literaturna Ukraina*, was pardoned from a five-year sentence of imprisonment.

While most of those arrested in Ukraine during the "General Pogrom" were involved in the burgeoning Ukrainian human and national rights movement or, as in the cases of Iurii Shukhevych and Danylo Shumuk, were former political prisoners, there were some exceptions. A number of young people were arrested and imprisoned for spontaneous acts of nationalistic defiance: Liubomyr Starosolsky and Roman Kolopach hoisted blue and yellow flags in May 1972 in the village of Stebnyk in the Lviv region;[25] in early 1973, seven youths replaced Soviet Ukrainian flags in the village of Rosokhach in the Ivano-Frankivsk region with blue and yellow ones.[26] In the same year, two students from Lviv, Zorian Popadiuk and Iaromyr Mykyta, were sentenced to 12 and 8 years imprisonment and internal exile respectively, for editing and circulating an unofficial nationalist journal entitled *Postup* among their colleagues.[27]

During the spring of 1973, the authorities discovered an underground nationalist organization known as the "Union of Ukrainian Youth of Halychyna" in the Ivano-Frankivsk region. Five young Ukrainians were arrested: Dmytro Hrinkiv, Mykola Motriuk, Ivan Shovkovy, Dmytro Dymidiv and Roman Chupry. They were charged with founding

> an illegal organization to fight against Soviet power for the secession of the Ukrainian SSR from the USSR and for the establishment of a so-called 'independent Ukraine,' by attracting new members into the above organization, by the ideological preparation and training of its members and of others in a spirit of anti-Soviet nationalism, and by establishing links with other organizations hostile to the Soviet Union, including ones abroad.[28]

At their trial in August 1973 the five defendants reportedly confessed that they had founded an anti-Soviet organization and stolen firearms and ammunition; sentences ranged from 5–7 years imprisonment.[29]

What then were the consequences of the "General Pogrom" for Ukrainian dissent? Undoubtedly, it had a traumatic effect, for not since the "Black Days" of the Zhdanov period had Ukrainian society experienced such a humiliating and blatantly anti-Ukrainian campaign of destruction and intimidation. First, the thoroughness of the KGB operation ensured that the key activists in Ukrainian dissent, and those associated with them, were rounded up, punished with long sentences of imprisonment, and dispatched "east" to the remote labour camp complexes of Mordovia and Perm. Others suspected of sympathizing with them were subjected to searches, interrogations, harassment and threats of dismissal from work, and made to witness the heavy penalties for involvement in dissenting activities. A striking example of the immense damage caused by the offensive was that after March 1972 the *Ukrainian Herald* failed to appear for two years. Second, the purge of the "Shelest faction" in the CPU destroyed any hopes the dissenters had of establishing a dialogue with the Soviet Ukrainian authorities, or of working within the official structures. In fact, the "General Pogrom" exposed the total incompatibility of the regime's goals and dissenters' demands. Moreover, the manifest official disregard for ideological and legal norms throughout the two-year period cast serious doubt on the feasibility and efficacy of the legalistic approach developed by Ukrainian dissenters since 1965.

The "General Pogrom" revealed other problems, too. Despite the open patriotic protest activity since the mid-sixties, Ukrainian dissent had been shown to be a relatively weak and vulnerable phenomenon lacking a definite political programme, adequate organization or a strong social base. Whatever national discontent may have existed among the Ukrainian population, and whatever the real or potential sympathy and support for the dissenters, Ukrainian dissent had not extended its roots from the intelligentsia to the working class and become a mass movement. It was still very much "a spontaneous, multiform, widespread, self-originating" movement of "national self-defense"[30] limited largely to the ranks of well-educated, first-generation urban dwellers. Kiev and Lviv were its two main centres. Although arrests had taken place in other major cities such as Kharkiv, Odessa and Dnipropetrovsk, there was a noticeable absence of dissenting activity in the highly urbanized and industrialized Donbas region. Also conspicuous was that despite the large number of Russians living in Ukraine—some 20 per cent of the republic's population—they took no part in the campaign for human rights, and offered no support to Ukrainian dissenters. On top of all this, outside the USSR there was a lack of awareness about, and interest in, Ukrainian dissent, which meant that the Soviet leadership's determination to crush it involved only a "negligible short-term political cost."[31]

The "General Pogrom" outraged Ukrainian dissenters and alienated them from the Soviet system. Over the next few years, anger, defiance and outspokenness characterized the numerous protests, statements and appeals prepared by those imprisoned in various penal institutions. Many renounced their Soviet citizenship, declared themselves to be Ukrainian separatists, and demanded recognition as political prisoners.[32] The fact that there was already a large number of Ukrainians in the camps serving sentences for "nationalist" activity only strengthened the new prisoners' belief that Ukrainian patriotism was regarded by the authorities as a crime.[33] The repressions of 1972–3 were interpreted as a national chastisement which, according to the poet Vasyl Stus, author of "I accuse," one of the most powerful protests of this period, had transformed an entire generation of the young Ukrainian intelligentsia into "a

generation of political prisoners," and inflicted "irreparable damage to the
Ukrainian nation and its culture."[34] The uncompromising stance adopted
by those imprisoned also manifested itself in their strong condemnation of
those former colleagues who had recanted.[35] In short, the "General
Pogrom" abruptly ended the patriotic protest phase in Ukrainian dissent
and ushered in a new one. The dissenters who had ended up in prisons and
labour camps now saw themselves as part of a Ukrainian national
opposition to Moscow's rule.

This "radicalization" was also demonstrated by the militant tone of the
Ukrainian Herald no. 7–8, which appeared in the spring of 1974. The
restrained and cautious editorial policy of the previous issues was
abandoned and the journal was given "a clearly defined political position"
of "uncompromising anti-colonialism." The editors explained that the
"trying times have toughened us even more and brought us closer
together." They declared that their aim was to "further unite around our
organ all democratic, anti-colonial groups in Ukraine, for it is only in this
direction that we can foresee progress in broadening the national liberation
struggle and the struggle for democracy."[36] Success was dependent on the
"mass dissemination of the free press" by both "external" and "internal"
means, through foreign radio broadcasts to the USSR and the commitment
and ingenuity of those within the country involved in this clandestine
activity.[37] Significantly, the editors did not reveal their names, nor the
names of the authors of two articles written expressly for the journal.
Having broken with the legalistic approach, they regarded the new
Ukrainian Herald as the mouthpiece of national opposition that had been
forced underground, dedicated to the overthrow of the Soviet regime and
to the achievement of an independent and democratic Ukrainian state.

Since the authorities had succeeded in largely destroying the *samvydav*
network in Ukraine, it is doubtful whether issue 7–8 of the *Ukrainian
Herald* was widely circulated. Nevertheless, it is an impressive document
of the Ukrainian national opposition. More than just a cry of anguish and
anger after a disastrous interlude, it represents a serious and frank attempt
to deal in political terms with the issues and problems confronting the
Ukrainian nation generally, and its dissidents in particular. It therefore
warrants closer inspection.

In the first part of the journal, the "Ukrainian problem" is considered
within the broad context of international relations. "Ukrainian democrats,"
while in favour of "international co-operation in all possible areas," warn
against the dire consequences for the "enslaved nations of the USSR" as
well as for the West, of naive, irresponsible "one-sided co-operation" that
would only strengthen the Soviet "fascist empire." The Soviet decision at
the beginning of the 1970s to embark on a policy of detente with the West
is seen as a consequence of the "crisis situation of the Soviet economy" and

the USSR's need for Western technological and economic assistance. The West is therefore urged to insist that co-operation of this kind be conditional on a Soviet undertaking to guarantee civil rights for its citizens.[38] The second part is devoted to a long discussion based on demographic statistics of what is described as "the colonial policy of Moscow's occupation forces in Ukraine." The journal employs far stronger language than Dziuba's celebrated critique of Soviet nationalities policy, and its attitude toward Lenin and his nationalities policy is unreservedly hostile. It charges the Soviet authorities with conducting a policy of forcible ethnocide of the non-Russian peoples. As recent evidence of this, the *Ukrainian Herald* provides a detailed and sombre account of the "General Pogrom" under the subheadings: "A Policy of Total Russification"; "The Purge of Party Cadres of the CPU"; "The Prohibition of Ukrainian Scholarship and Culture"; "The Persecution of the Intelligentsia"; "The Destruction of Ukrainian Historical and Cultural Monuments"; "The Destruction of Churches and Persecution of the Faithful." The journal ends with an appeal to the United Nations to condemn "Soviet-Russian colonialism."[39]

The *Ukrainian Herald* no. 7–8 explicitly recognized the importance of making the "Ukrainian problem" known outside the Soviet Union and of securing the sympathy and support of international public opinion. The editors, evidently aware that decolonization had been a major issue in international politics after the Second World War, appear to have deliberately presented their cause as one of "uncompromising anti-colonialism" in order to ensure that the nature of their struggle would be clearly understood.[40] They also attached great importance to the role of the Ukrainian "diaspora" and even appealed to the UN to give the World Congress of Free Ukrainians "the right to represent the interests of the Ukrainian people" until democratic elections could be held in Ukraine.[41] Other interesting aspects of this *samvydav* journal are its critique of the "existing order in the USSR" as having "nothing in common with socialism," and its sympathetic attitude toward Soviet Jewry and courageous Russian critics of the Soviet regime like Sakharov and Solzhenitsyn.

The identities of those responsible for the preparation of the *Ukrainian Herald* no. 7–8 were only revealed with their arrests in the spring of 1980. The main editor and author was Stepan Khmara, a stomatologist and former trade union official working in the Lviv region. He was aided by Vitalii Shevchenko, a former KGB officer, party member and journalist, and Oleksander Shevchenko, a journalist. Both worked in Kiev. Khmara is reported to have prepared a ninth issue of the *Ukrainian Herald* although this apparently had not been disseminated. Khmara was charged with the preparation not only of issues 7–8 and 9 of the *Ukrainian Herald*, but also of the less militant sixth number.[42] Issue 7–8, therefore, was not prepared by a representative of a wholly different breed of Ukrainian dissent, but by a hitherto unknown activist who had been involved in the compilation of an earlier issue.

For several years after the "General Pogrom" there was virtually no open national dissent in Ukraine, though political arrests continued.[43] This did not mean, however, that the authorities had eliminated Ukrainian dissent, but rather that they had driven it underground. In the spring of 1974, for instance, a number of people were arrested in Horodenka, in the Ivano-Frankivsk region, in connection with the preparation and dissemination of *samvydav*.[44] In the following year, Vitalii Tyshchenko, a 34-year-old Ukrainian from the Kharkiv region is reported to have been imprisoned for organizing an underground printing-press to produce *samvydav*.[45] The case of Iurii Badzio a philologist and dissenter, who from 1972 until his arrest in April 1979 worked secretly on a mammoth critical study of the consequences of Soviet nationalities policy in Ukraine, did not become known until much later.[46]

There were also indications that in Western Ukraine, as in the 1960s, underground, non-violent, nationalist groups continued to be formed. In late 1974 or early 1975, the authorities discovered a clandestine nationalist group known as the "National-Democratic Liberation Union 'Homin'" in the Ivano-Frankivsk region. One of its members, Mykola Slobodian, a former lieutenant in the militia, was tried in July 1975 and sentenced to a total of eleven years imprisonment and internal exile. The fate of his colleagues, who included V. Slobodian, V. Melnychuk, L. Melnychuk and I. Myroniak, is not known.[47] Not long after the arrest of the members of the "Homin" group, another clandestine organization calling itself the "Ukrainian National Front" was formed in the same region. At its peak it is reported to have contained up to forty members. Its main purpose appears to have been the preparation and circulation of *samvydav*. The group is reported to have published two issues each of a literary almanac, *Prozrinia* and a journal called the *Ukrainian Herald*. The Ukrainian National Front had no connections with an organization of the same name active in the Ivano-Frankivsk region from 1964 to 1967, nor was its journal the *Ukrainian Herald* the same as Khmara's publication. The group apparently continued its activities for several years until the arrest of three of its members in 1979.[48]

In the aftermath of the General Pogrom, as distressing reports about conditions and protests filtered out from the places of imprisonment, the relatives of political prisoners petitioned the authorities and publicized the information. One of the most active campaigners was Oksana Meshko, a former political prisoner during the Stalin era, who managed to persuade not only Ivan Dziuba, but also a deputy of the Supreme Soviet of the

Ukrainian SSR, Mykhailo Stelmakh, to intervene, albeit unsuccessfully, on behalf of her son Oleksander Serhiienko.[49] Friends and sympathizers of political prisoners attempted to provide material assistance to their families. In October 1974, for example, Oksana Popovych, an invalid and like Meshko, a former political prisoner, was arrested in Ivano-Frankivsk and subsequently sentenced to a total of 13 years imprisonment and internal exile for distributing *samvydav* and collecting money "to pay for the defense of Ukrainian political prisoners."[50]

In Russia where the 1972 crackdown on dissent had been less damaging, the situation was more encouraging. As Peter Reddaway has noted, "for the mainstream human rights movement the years 1974–76 saw relatively few losses and an impressive growth in the *Chronicle....* "[51] Valuable information on the situation of Ukrainian political prisoners appeared regularly in this *samvydav* journal. Moreover, in a number of cases, Russian human rights activists played important roles in publicizing the plight of individual Ukrainian dissidents and in assisting their families. In 1974, for example, when Valentyn Moroz went on a long hunger strike in protest against his conditions of confinement, Andrei Sakharov, Malva Landa and Tatiana Khodorovich spoke out in his defence.[52] In the same year, together with Elena Bonner, Tatiana Velikanova, Sergei Kovalev, Andrei Tverdokhlebov, Iurii Orlov and others, they issued appeals on behalf of Leonid Pliushch.[53] Both of these cases attracted considerable attention in the West, where campaigns were launched in support of both men. Reports about the hardships borne by Ukrainian political prisoners and their courageous behaviour led to an unprecedented mobilization of the Ukrainian diaspora during the mid-1970s in defence of imprisoned Ukrainian dissidents.

Gradually, new figures began to emerge in Ukrainian dissent. Ukrainian literary life had been affected more directly by arrests and the tightening of ideological controls than most other sectors, and in the mid-1970s two well known and prolific writers joined the ranks of the dissidents. In 1974 the prose writer and poet Mykola Rudenko, a decorated war invalid and former high ranking official in the Writers Union of Ukraine became acquainted with Andrei Sakharov, Valentin Turchin and Iurii Orlov, and subsequently joined the Moscow-based group of Amnesty International. This and his authorship of a philosophical and economic critique of Marxism entitled *Economic Monologues* led to harassment by the authorities, including expulsion from the Writers Union, short-term detention and confinement in a psychiatric hospital for two months.[54] His colleague, the science fiction writer and poet Oles Berdnyk, who had been expelled from the Writers Union in 1972, wrote a number of patriotic works which circulated in *samvydav* and eventually were published in the West.[55] While Rudenko through his involvement in the Soviet Amnesty

International group became identified as a human rights campaigner, Berdnyk unsuccessfully sought permission to emigrate from the Soviet Union. At the end of 1975, several leading Ukrainian dissidents, the lawyers Levko Lukianenko and Ivan Kandyba, and the microbiologist Nina Strokata-Karavanska, were released from imprisonment on expiry of their sentences. Although impeded by official restrictions and distance—Strokata-Karavanska was under administrative surveillance in the Kaluga region, Lukianenko in Chernihiv and Kandyba in the Lviv region, together with Rudenko, Berdnyk and Meshko, who were based in Kiev—they gradually managed to form a new nucleus around which Ukrainian dissent was to coalesce.

The new form of Ukrainian dissent was inspired by developments on the international scene and the Russian human rights movement's response to them. In the summer of 1975, the situation hoped for by the editor of the *Ukrainian Herald* 7–8 began to take shape. The signing in August of the 'Final Act' of the 35-nation European Conference on Security and Co-operation in Helsinki formally linked the question of human rights to a major international agreement. Having promoted the idea of a European security conference as a substitute for a European peace conference, the Soviet Union obtained recognition of the status quo in Europe, that is, acceptance of its post-Second World War territorial and political gains in Eastern Europe, at the cost of agreeing to observe basic human rights. Moreover, provisions were also included in the Helsinki Final Act for the monitoring and review of compliance with these undertakings.

The Helsinki Final Act not only raised expectations among Soviet human rights campaigners, but more important, presented new opportunities for open activity. After all, as Liudmilla Alekseiieva has pointed out, "the humanitarian clauses of the Helsinki accord were the first international agreements on human rights to be published in the Soviet press."[56] In October, Soviet dissenters were further heartened by the announcement that Andrei Sakharov had been awarded the Nobel Peace Prize. In the same month, the French Communist Party joined the escalating Western campaign to free Leonid Pliushch from psychiatric confinement. In January 1976, Pliushch was suddenly freed and allowed to leave the Soviet Union. At this juncture the Soviet authorities were clearly sensitive and responsive to Western criticism of human rights violations in their country.

Against this promising background, on 12 May 1976, eleven human rights campaigners announced the formation of a new human rights organization in Moscow—the Public Group to Promote the Implementation of the Helsinki Accords in the USSR. The organizers stated that the aim of the group was to "promote observance of the humanitarian provisions of the Final Act of the Conference on

Co-operation and Security in Europe." They declared their intention to gather information on violations of the human rights provisions of the Final Act, to process this material and to communicate it to the governments and public of the signatory states. Proceeding from the conviction that "the issues of humanitarianism and free information have a direct relationship to the problem of international security," the founding members called on the public of signatory states to form their own national Helsinki monitoring groups "in order to assist a complete fulfilment of the Helsinki Agreements" by their governments.[57] When the authorities responded to the formation of the Moscow Helsinki Group by attacking it as an "illegal organization," its leader, Iurii Orlov, issued an appeal addressed to "the governments and parliaments" of states which signed the Helsinki Final Act asking them to "take steps which will protect the right of the Group to Promote Observances of the Helsinki Accords to function in a reasonable and constructive fashion in conformity with its stated purposes."[58]

Over the next few months, the Moscow Helsinki group achieved considerable success in documenting and publicizing a broad range of human rights violations in the Soviet Union and became an attractive model for Ukrainian dissidents.[59] The materials issued by the Moscow Helsinki monitors contained considerable information about Ukrainian political prisoners, former political prisoners, religious believers and would-be emigrants. In the summer of 1976, Moscow Helsinki group member Alexander Ginzburg and Soviet Amnesty International group member Valentin Turchin travelled to Lviv to meet the family of the Ukrainian political prisoner Ivan Hel,[60] and during their stay in Western Ukraine are reported to have discussed with some Ukrainian dissidents the need to establish a Ukrainian Helsinki monitoring group. Meanwhile in Kiev, Mykola Rudenko, who was in close touch with prominent human rights campaigners in Moscow, became the leading proponent of such a group.

Sensing the opportunities offered by the Helsinki Final Act, and stimulated by the example of the Moscow Helsinki monitoring group, Ukrainian dissidents for the first time made an attempt to establish a human rights organization that would be a focus and a forum for Ukrainian dissent. The initiators were well aware that the 'Ukrainian question' hardly figured in the world of international politics. The Ukrainian Soviet Socialist Republic, though formally a sovereign state with its own seat at the UN, had after all not even participated in the Conference on Co-operation and Security in Europe. The establishment of a Ukrainian Helsinki monitoring group, they hoped, would make the struggle for human and national rights in Ukraine part of the Helsinki process and, by drawing international attention for the first time to this problem, would reduce Ukraine's isolation.

On 9 November 1976, Rudenko, Berdnyk, Lukianenko, Kandyba, Strokata-Karavanska, Meshko and four others announced the formation of the Ukrainian Public Group to Promote the Implementation of the Helsinki Accords.[61] The founding members affirmed their commitment to the Universal Declaration of Human Rights, as well as the human rights provisions of the Helsinki Final Act. In addition, however, they emphasized their concern for the national aspect by stating that they considered it illegal that "Ukraine, a full member of the UN, was not represented by a separate delegation" at the Helsinki Conference. The group aimed "to promote the familiarization of wide circles of the Ukrainian public with the Declaration of Human Rights"; "to promote actively the implementation of the humanitarian articles" of the Helsinki Final Act; "to demand that Ukraine, as a sovereign European state and member of the UN, be represented by its own delegation at all international conferences" dealing with the implementation of the Helsinki Accords; and "to demand the accreditation in Ukraine of the foreign press, the creation of independent news agencies and the like." The "primary task" of the group was defined as "informing the governments of the participating countries and the world public about violations in Ukraine of the Universal Declaration of Human Rights and the humanitarian articles accepted by the Helsinki Conference." To this end the group would accept written complaints about such violations, compile information on "the state of legality in Ukraine," study the infringement of the human rights of Ukrainians living in other republics of the USSR, and do its utmost to publicize the findings. The organizers explained that the group's activities would be motivated not by political, but by humanitarian and legal considerations.[62]

Two days later, the group's leader Mykola Rudenko and another member, Petro Hryhorenko, announced that the latter "in response to like-minded Ukrainian colleagues" had agreed to become the group's representative in Moscow.[63] This was a considerable success for the Ukrainian Helsinki Group, for Hryhorenko, a former Major-General in the Red Army who had become one of the best known and respected Soviet human rights campaigners, although a Ukrainian, had not previously been directly associated with Ukrainian dissent. His membership was important not only because of his reputation, but because it provided the group with a spokesman in the Soviet capital. The other three founding members of the Ukrainian Helsinki group were Oleksii Tykhy, a teacher from Donetsk and a former political prisoner, and two young dissenters from the Kiev region, Mykola Matusevych, a historian, and Myroslav Marynovych, an electrical engineer.

The group's membership was made up of representatives of various generations and people of very different backgrounds ranging from the seasoned national rights campaigners and former organizers of a clandestine national-democratic group in the early 1960s, Lukianenko and Kandyba, to the young newcomers to dissent, Marynovych and Matusevych. Alongside former political prisoners of the Stalin era, Berdnyk, Meshko and Tykhy, were a former high-ranking Communist Party official, Rudenko, and a former Red Army general, Hryhorenko. Nina Strokata-Karavanska, a much respected human rights campaigner in her own right, was moreover the wife of one of the best known and longest serving Ukrainian political prisoners, Sviatoslav Karavansky. The group was, therefore, a veritable microcosm of Ukrainian dissent and represented an attempt to create a unified structure in which ideological and tactical differences would be submerged.

The formation of the Ukrainian Helsinki monitoring group was not only enthusiastically greeted by the Moscow group, but also occasioned an unprecedented statement about Ukraine from six leading Moscow human rights campaigners:

> Ignoring the fact that Ukraine is formally a member of the United Nations with full rights, it was not invited to the conference in Belgrade; there are no Western correspondents based in its capital; in fact there are also no diplomatic representatives there, that could be given information.... Considering the conditions existing in Ukraine, the creation of the Ukrainian Public Group is an act of great courage.[64]

Pledging wholehearted support for their Ukrainian colleagues, the Russian dissidents, all members of the Moscow Helsinki group, appealed to world opinion not to let the Ukrainian group "out of its sight."[65] That this juncture marked a pinnacle in relations between Ukrainian and Russian dissidents was underlined shortly afterward in Document no. 12 of the Moscow Helsinki group, which stressed that "Ukrainians have constituted and constitute today a very substantial part of the contingent of prisoners of conscience, disproportionately greater than the percentage of that nation in the USSR's population."[66] The examples set by the Moscow and Ukrainian groups were followed in other areas of the Soviet Union. Other Helsinki groups were formed in Lithuania (November 1976), Georgia (January 1977) and Armenia (April 1977).

In their first two *Memoranda*, dated November-December 1976 and 20 January 1977 respectively, the Ukrainian Helsinki monitors provided further information about the aims and concerns of their group. Most of *Memorandum* no. 1 was devoted to a detailed description of the situation in Ukraine. Particularly telling was that in a section headed "Typical Violations of Human Rights," the authors treated human rights and national rights as inseparable concepts. In a tone rather reminiscent of the *Ukrainian Herald* no. 7–8, they argued that "from the first years of the

Stalinist dictatorship Ukraine became the scene of genocide and ethnocide" and consequently "the national rights of Ukraine as a member of the [Soviet] Union ceased to be a social reality." Therefore, despite official claims to the contrary, the nationalities problem in Ukraine was paramount. "Fanatical great power chauvinists" were behind the continuing cases of imprisonment or psychiatric confinement of Ukrainian patriots. The authors underscored their argument by presenting details of over eighty Ukrainian political prisoners ranging from cultural activists arrested in 1972 to former participants in the armed resistance struggle waged by the Organization of Ukrainian Nationalists and the Ukrainian Insurgent Army in the 1940s.[67] *Memorandum* no. 2 was concerned with the question of Ukraine's participation in the forthcoming Belgrade conference to review the implementation of the Helsinki Final Act. Security in Europe," the authors argued, could not "become a reality if a nation of fifty million," which had suffered through countless misfortunes during the two world wars, "is artificially kept from participating in European affairs." The document ended with an oblique statement to the effect that the threat of a new world war could only be averted if the nations of Eastern Europe achieved full independence and that therefore it was in the West's interest to promote this.[68]

In early February, the authorities made their first major move against the Moscow and Ukrainian Helsinki Groups. Two members of the Moscow group, Iurii Orlov, the chairman, and Alexander Ginzburg were arrested. In Ukraine on 5 February, Mykola Rudenko and Oleksii Tykhy were also arrested. Other members of the Ukrainian group were subjected to searches. Four days later, however, members of the latter jointly issued their *Memorandum* no. 4, entitled "On New Repressions in Ukraine Against Members of the Helsinki Group," in which they appealed to world public opinion to support their arrested colleagues.[69] Less than a week later, they again demonstrated their determination by issuing their most outspoken document to date—*Memorandum* no. 5, entitled "Ukraine of the Summer of 1977," which was also the first to contain programmatic elements.

Memorandum no. 5, addressed to the countries participating in the Belgrade review conference, dealt in unequivocal terms with the question of Ukraine's statehood. "Let us not be playing blindman's bluff" the authors declared:

> This statehood of ours is nothing but a paper mirage. And the time has come to dot all the "i's," to end the incessant and insidious game with our sovereignty, as well as with the sovereignty of all the other Union republics.... Why should Ukraine's cultural, creative, scientific, agricultural and international problems be defined and planned in the capital of the

neighbouring (even if allied) state? We are not naive simpletons. We understand that at work here is [the] spirit of imperialism and chauvinism. . . . [70]

The Soviet authorities were urged to respect Ukraine's right to self-determination, and to a sovereign spiritual life, as well as the human rights of its citizens. The Ukrainian people, as well as all the other nations comprising the USSR, the authors insisted, "should be masters of their land, their tradition, their creative inheritance, their . . . aspirations, their will to build a better life for each, for all."

The Ukrainian Helsinki members demanded the following: an amnesty for all political prisoners and the end of political imprisonment in the Soviet Union; the removal of the system of censorship; the free flow of information; recognition of the right to freedom of expression; freedom of association and freedom of movement; the abolition of the death penalty; the rejection of violence and militarism; and greater international co-operation in dealing with the pressing economic, ecological and demographic problems facing mankind. [71]

As a political manifesto, *Memorandum* no. 5 is marred by the inclusion of poetic and utopian elements, unmistakably the work of Oles Berdnyk, for all his good intentions, a man of literature and science fiction, not of politics. The document is nevertheless a landmark in the development of Ukrainian dissent because it represents the first real attempt to formulate a political programme of the Ukrainian human and national rights movement. Although its proposals were already implicit in Ukrainian dissenting thought of the preceding decade, they had never been expressed so forthrightly and clearly. Now there existed a programmatic document, however rudimentary, which defined the minimal goals of Ukrainian human and national rights campaigners. Over the next two years, the crystallization of Ukrainian dissenting thought precipitated by *Memorandum* no. 5 and the other initial documents of the Ukrainian Helsinki monitoring group, was to continue. Oles Berdnyk, Father Vasyl Romaniuk together with Oleksii Tykhy, and Iurii Lytvyn and the Ukrainian Patriotic Movement all later helped to develop the programme of Ukrainian dissent. [72]

The formation of the Ukrainian Helsinki monitoring group marked an important new stage in the development of Ukrainian dissent. In place of the amorphous movement in defence of Ukrainian cultural and national identity that had existed prior to 1972, there now emerged the fully crystallized nucleus of a human and national rights movement. The organizers of the Ukrainian group, while defining their "mission" as "a movement in defence of rights" (*pravozakhysnyi rukh*) and "the rule of law," saw themselves as a continuation of the Ukrainian national movement and boldly pointed this out in their documents. They realized that success was dependent on their ability both to broaden the base of dissent in Ukraine through "the development of legal consciousness" in society, and to reduce the international isolation of Ukraine.[73] As members of the first Ukrainian human rights organization, the Ukrainian Helsinki monitors modelled their group as much on the Initiative Group for Human Rights in the USSR and the Committee for Human Rights as they did on the Moscow Helsinki group. Basing their activity on international human rights norms, they sought on the one hand to educate the Ukrainian public about its rights,[74] and on the other, to publicize Ukraine's situation before the international community.

Within five years of the launching of the "General Pogrom," Ukrainian dissent had resurfaced in a different form. This period saw a shift from cultural and largely apolitical patriotic protest activity to political opposition. The Ukrainian Helsinki monitoring group epitomized this trend, its programmatic position reflecting the democratic, national ideological orientation dominating Ukrainian dissidence in both its overt and covert activity. Ironically, just as the arrests of Ukrainian intellectuals in 1965 had stimulated rather than retarded the development of dissent, so the major repressive drive of 1972–3 not only failed to eliminate this phenomenon but served as the catalyst for the appearance of a more mature strain of open dissidence with an incipient organizational structure and defined political goals.

Notes

1. On Ukrainian dissent prior to Shelest's ouster see, for example, M. Browne, ed., *Ferment in the Ukraine* (London 1971); T. Szamuely, "The Resurgence of Ukrainian Nationalism," *The Reporter*, 30 May 1968, 15–18; J. Birch, "The Ukrainian Nationalist Movement in the USSR since 1956," *Ukrainian Review* 4 (1970): 2–47; V. Swoboda, "Cat and Mouse in the Ukraine," *Index on Censorship* 2, no. 1 (1973): 81–9; B. Bociurkiw, "Soviet Nationalities Policy and Dissent in the Ukraine," *The World Today* (May 1974): 214–26; G. Liber and A. Mostovych, eds., *Nonconformity and Dissent in the Ukrainian SSR 1955–1975: An Annotated Bibliography* (Cambridge 1978) and K. C. Farmer, *Ukrainian Nationalism in the Post-Stalin Era: Myth, Symbols and Ideology in Soviet Nationalities Policy* (The Hague, Boston and London 1980).

2. P. Reddaway, "The Development of Dissent and Opposition," in *The Soviet Union Since the Fall of Khrushchev*, ed. A. Brown and M. Kaser (London and Basingstoke 1978), 35.

3. The *samvydav* human rights journal *A Chronicle of Current Events*, no. 25 (dated 20 May 1972), for instance, published an unconfirmed report that there had been more than 100 arrests in Ukraine between January and May

1972. (English language translations of this journal since issue no. 16 have been published in London by Amnesty International Publications. They will be referred to hereafter as *Chronicle*.) According to the Ukrainian *samvydav* journal the *Ukrainian Herald*, no. 7–8 (dated Spring 1974) even this figure was far off the mark. *Ukrainian Herald Issue 7–8: Ethnocide of Ukrainians in the USSR* (Baltimore 1976), 138.

4. *Ukrainian Herald Issue 7–8*, 125–61.

5. See J. Pelenski, "Shelest and His Period in Soviet Ukraine (1962–1972): A Revival of Controlled Ukrainian Autonomism" and Y. Bilinsky, "The Communist Party of Ukraine After 1966," in *Ukraine in the Seventies*, ed. P. J. Potichnyj (Oakville 1975), 283–307 and 239–55 respectively. Also G. Hodnett, "The Views of Petro Shelest," *Annals of the Ukrainian Academy of Arts and Sciences in the U.S.* 14, no. 37–8 (1978–1980): 209–43.

6. The first two issues were published together in book form in Ukrainian under the title *Ukrainskyi visnyk, Vypusk 1–11* (Paris and Baltimore 1970).

7. See "A Statement Regarding the Formation of A Citizens' Committee for the Defense of Nina Strokata," in *Dissent in Ukraine: Ukrainian Herald, Issue 6*, ed. and trans., L. Jones and B. Yasen (Baltimore-Paris-Toronto 1977), 141–3.

8. *Ukrainskyi visnyk. Vypusk III* (Baltimore-Winnipeg 1971), 77.

9. *Chronicle*, no. 22 (dated 10 November 1971), 44–6. Issue 5 of the *Ukrainian Herald* has not reached the West. *Chronicle*, no. 22, however, reproduced in abridged form the editorial statement on the question.

10. "Z pryvodu lysta Borysa Kovhara" (dating from 1972) in *Pohrom v Ukraini: 1972–1979*, ed. R. Kupchinsky (New York 1980), 202.

11. B. Kovhar, "Vidkrytyi lyst" (dated 1 February 1972) in *Pohrom v Ukraini*, 189–202. See also *Chronicle*, no. 28 (dated 31 December 1972), 28–9.

12. *Ukrainian Herald Issue 6*, 19.

13. *Chronicle*, no. 25 (dated 20 May 1972), 180–1.

14. *Chronicle*, no. 26 (dated 5 July 1972), 243–4.

15. V. Lisovy and I. Proniuk, "Vidkrytyi lyst do chleniv TsK KPRS," in *Pohrom v Ukraini*, 167–85. For an English translation of the protest, see V. Lisovy, *Open Letter to the CPSU* (Edmonton 1978).

16. Ibid., 175–81.

17. On Ivan Dziuba see "Ivan Mikhailovich Dziuba," *Radio Free Europe Research*, Communist Area, no. 1775, 25 April 1973; also M. Savaryn, "Why Capitulate?: Ivan Dziuba's Trauma," *Journal Of Ukrainian Graduate Studies*, no. 3 (Fall 1977): 54–61.

18. *Chronicle*, no. 25, 177–8.

19. See Pelenski, "Shelest and His Period," and Hodnett, "The Views of Petro Shelest," and L. Tillet, "Ukrainian Nationalism and the Fall of Shelest," *Slavic Review* 34, no. 4 (December 1975): 752–68.

20. See the report on the press conference in *Chronicle*, no. 26, 244–5.

21. *Chronicle*, no. 27 (dated 15 October 1972), 278 and 282.

22. Ibid., 278–9. See also the various documents about Serhiienko's case in *Pohrom v Ukraini*, 138–66.

23. *Chronicle*, no. 27, 286–7.

24. *Ukrainian Herald Issue 7–8*, 145–8. See also *Chronicle*, no. 28, 32.

25. *Pohrom v Ukraini*, 18.

26. See *Chronicle*, no. 47 (dated 30 November 1977), 144 and *Suchasnist*, no. 2 (1977): 94–8.

27. *The Ukrainian Herald Issue 7–8*, 140 and *Pohrom v Ukraini*, 17. According to Mikhail Kheifets, who met Popadiuk in a labour camp, the students belonged to an underground nationalist organization called the "Ukrainian National-Liberation Front," which contained several dozen members, mainly university and high school students. See *Suchasnist*, no. 10 (1980): 70–6. Elsewhere, Kheifets has provided a brief but illuminating account of how Popadiuk became involved in oppositional activity. See M. Kheifets, *Mesto i vremia* (Paris 1978): 117–18.

28. *Chronicle*, no. 33 (dated 10 December 1974), 176–8 and *Suchasnist*, no. 5 (1975): 116–17.

29. *Chronicle*, no. 33, 178–9. There have been unconfirmed reports that the attempt to create an 'armed' nationalist group was a KGB provocation designed to discredit Ukrainian dissent.

30. I. Dzyuba, *Internationalism or Russification?* (New York 1974), 204.

31. P. Reddaway, "Policy towards Dissent since Khrushchev" in *Authority, Power and Policy in the USSR: Essays dedicated to Leonard Schapiro*, ed., T. H. Rigby, A. Brown and P. Reddaway (London and Basingstoke 1980), 172–3.

32. See for example Viacheslav Chornovil's statement of 1 March 1975, entitled "I renounce my citizenship" in *Index on Censorship* 5, no. 1 (Spring 1976): 62.

33. See ibid. and Vasyl Stus' statement, "Do Prezidii Verkhovnoi Rady URSR" (dated 1 August 1976), *Pohrom v Ukraini*, 47.

34. V. Stus, "Ia obvynuvachuiuu" (dated 1975), *Pohrom v Ukraini*, 40–4. Stus later wrote that "Until January 1972 I was a Ukrainophile (I think most of my friends were of the same hue). Mordovia made me a Ukrainian. Now I am unpeturbed how they label me: a nationalist, spy or traitor. I know that my spiritual life and that of my nation are too catastrophic for me to sit quietly with my arms folded." "Lyst do pryiateliv" (dated 29 October 1977), *Pohrom v Ukraini*, 50.

35. See, for instance, I. Kalynets, "Pokhoron druha—(svitska khronika)" (dated 20 June 1976), *Pohrom v Ukraini*, 246–9; V. Stus, "Vidkrytyi lyst do Ivana Dziuby," ibid., 44–6; I. Svitlychny, "Vidkrytyi lyst Mykoli Bazhanu" (dated December 1976), ibid., 108–22; and V. Chornovil, "Lyst do N.N.," *Suchasnist*, no. 11 (1976): 87–9.

36. *Ukrainian Herald Issue 7–8*, 15.

37. Ibid.

38. Ibid., 19–33.

39. Ibid., 160.
40. Ibid., 15.
41. Ibid., 160.
42. Khmara, was a former member of an official local trade union council and had sought to improve working conditions for his colleagues. His party membership was blocked and he was forced to give up his trade union activities. Vitalii Shevchenko was a former KGB officer and party member. He had worked for the Radio and Telegraphic Agency of Ukraine (RATAU) in Kiev and at the time of his arrest was employed in the technical information department of a factory. Oleksandr Shevchenko was chief secretary of the editorial board of the *Ukrainian Biochemical Journal*. See *Chronicle*, no. 60 (dated 31 December 1980), 52–9 and *USSR News Briefs*, no. 2, 31 (January 1981), 2–3.
43. In 1974, for example, two Ukrainian former political prisoners, Bohdan Rebryk and Iurii Lytvyn were arrested and charged with possessing and circulating *samvydav*. Rebryk was sentenced to a total of fifteen years imprisonment and internal exile. Lytvyn was sentenced to three years imprisonment. On the circumstances of Rebryk's arrest, see Rebryk's letter to George Meany in *Workers Against the Gulag*, ed. V. Haynes and O. Semyonova (London 1979), 95–7. On Lytvyn see *Chronicles*, no. 39 (12 March 1976) and 46 (15 August 1977). There were also three notable cases involving individual protesters. At the end of January 1976, Ievhen Kramar, a jurist from the Volyn region addressed an appeal to Communist Parties in the West protesting against human rights violations in the USSR and persecution of him by the authorities. (See *Suchasnist*, no. 1 (1977): 103–6.) During the same year, Leonid Siry, a worker from Odessa seeking to emigrate from the Soviet Union with his large family, wrote several appeals to the authorities. In his "Open Letter" of 14 November 1976 he not only described the poor standard of living his family was subjected to, but also made a series of demands. These included an end to restrictions of individual liberties and civil rights; independent trade unions, genuine elections to all positions of political power and the restoration and expansion of the rights of the national republics (see *Workers Against the Gulag*, 98–116). In December 1976, Iosyp Terelia, a Ukrainian Uniate Catholic and former political prisoner, sent a strongly worded open letter to Iurii Andropov, the Chairman of the KGB, in which he protested against the persecution of Ukrainian Catholics and the abuse of psychiatry for political purposes in the Soviet Union. See Y. Terelya, *Notes from a Madhouse*, ed. and trans. B. Yasen (Baltimore-Washington-Toronto 1977).
44. *Chronicle*, no. 34 (dated 31 December 1974), 23.
45. *USSR News Brief: Spisok Politzakliuchennykh SSSR (po sostoianiiu na 1.5.1981)*, ed. K. Liubarski (Brussels 1981).
46. Iu. Badzio, *Vidkrytyi lyst do Prezydii Verkhovnoi Rady Soiuzu RSR ta Tsentralnoho komitetu KPRS* (New York 1980).
47. *Chronicle*, no. 52 (dated 1 March 1979), 104.
48. On the Ukrainian National Front, see *Chronicle*, no. 60, 51–2, *Arkhiv*

Samizdata, document no. 4233, entitled "Ishche iz istorii UNF" published by Radio Liberty, Munich and ZP UHVR Press Release no. 10/81, 30 March 1981. The three arrested were Mykola Krainyk, a former history teacher, Vasyl Zvarych and Ivan Mandryk. Krainyk was arrested in September 1979 and sentenced in August 1980 to ten years imprisonment and three years of internal exile for "anti-Soviet agitation and propaganda" and "participation in an anti-Soviet organization." Zvarych was convicted on the basis of a trumped-up charge of "hooliganism" and sentenced to two and a half years imprisonment. Mandryk, reportedly the most active member of the UNF, disappeared mysteriously one day and his wife was eventually shown his beaten-up and knifed body by the authorities, and told that he had committed suicide by jumping out of the fifth-floor window of a hotel in Ivano-Frankivsk.

49. *Pohrom v Ukraini*, 148–54.

50. *Chronicle*, no. 34, 23–4.

51. P. Reddaway, "Policy towards Dissent since Khrushchev," 175.

52. See *A Chronicle of Human Rights in the USSR* (New York), no. 8 (March-April 1974), 15–17 and 9 (May-June 1974), 36–8, and *Chronicles*, no. 33 and no. 34.

53. See, for instance, *Chronicle*, no. 32 (dated 17 July 1974), 99, *Chronicle*, no. 34, 39 and 74. Tatiana Khodorovich also compiled a collection of documents about Pliushch's case entitled *Istoriia bolezni Leonida Pliushcha* (Amsterdam 1974). Another example of Russian activists speaking out on behalf of a Ukrainian political prisoner at this time was the case of Father Vasyl Romaniuk. See Documents 19–22 in *Vasyl Romanyuk: A Voice in the Wilderness*, ed. and trans. J. Dobczansky (Wheaton, Illinois 1980), 87–95.

54. On Rudenko, see P. Grigorenko, "My Friend Mykola Rudenko," *Index on Censorship* 8, no. 1 (January-February 1979): 33–40.

55. On Berdnyk, see J. Dobczansky, "Oles Berdnyk: A Bibliographical Overview," *Journal of Ukrainian Graduate Studies* 4, no. 1 (Spring 1979): 77–83.

56. L. Alexeyeva, "The Human Rights Movement in the USSR," *Survey* 23, no. 4 (Autumn 1977–78): 74.

57. See the declaration of 12 May 1976 entitled, "The Founding of the Public Group to Promote Observance of the Helsinki Accords in the USSR" in *Documents of the Helsinki Watch Group in the USSR*, Number One (New York 1977), vii–viii.

58. Iu. Orlov, "An Appeal to the Governments and Parliaments of States which signed the Final Act of the Conference on Security and Cooperation in Europe," *Documents of the Helsinki Watch Group in the USSR*, Number One, ix–x.

59. On the early activity of the Moscow Helsinki monitoring group, see the various documents it published in *Documents of the Helsinki Watch Group in the USSR*, Numbers One and Two.

60. *Chronicle*, no. 43 (dated 31 December 1976).

61. "Declaration of the Ukrainian Public Group to Promote the Implementation of the Helsinki Accords," 9 November 1976, in *The Human Rights Movement in Ukraine: Documents of the Ukrainian Helsinki Group 1976–1980*, ed. L. Verba and B. Yasen (Baltimore, Washington, Toronto 1980), 19–22. This collection will subsequently be referred to as *Documents of the Ukrainian Helsinki Group*.

62. Ibid., 20–1. Rudenko sought to elucidate the distinct character of the Ukrainian Helsinki group in his open letter of 14 November addressed "to people of good will." Reiterating that the group had humanitarian rather than political goals, he emphasized that it "cannot avoid the nationality question: most Ukrainian political prisoners have been sentenced for imagined or real nationalism. And it is precisely this Ukrainian nationalism that the government which considers itself Soviet fears most." Moreover, he firmly rejected the idea that the Ukrainian group was a "branch" of the Moscow Helsinki group, saying that "our relations are built on friendship and co-operation, not subordination." See *Documents of the Ukrainian Helsinki Group*, 139–42.

63. "Notice of the formation of the Ukrainian Public Group to Promote the Implementation of the Helsinki Accords," 11 November 1976, *Documents of the Ukrainian Helsinki Group*, 23.

64. "Povidomlennia: Pro stvorennia Ukrainskoi hromadskoi hrupy spryiannia vykonanniu Helsinskykh uhod," dated 12 November 1976 in *Ukrainskyi pravozakhysnyi rykh: Dokumenty i materiialy Kyivskoi ukrainskoi hrupy spryiannia vykonanniu Helsinskykh uhod*, comp. O. Zinkevych (Baltimore and Toronto 1978), 10.

65. Ibid.

66. Document no. 12 of the Moscow Helsinki Monitoring Group, dated December 1976 in *Documents of the Helsinki Watch Group in the USSR*, Number Two, 34–5.

67. *Memorandum no. 1:* "The Effects of the European Conference on the Development of Legal Consciousness in Ukraine," November-December 1976, *Documents of the Ukrainian Helsinki Group*, 46–53.

68. *Memorandum no. 2:* "Concerning the Participation of Ukraine in the Belgrade Conference, 1977," 20 January 1977, *Documents of the Ukrainian Helsinki Group*, 64.

69. *Memorandum no. 4:* "On New Repressions in Ukraine Against Members of the Helsinki Group," 9 February 1977, *Documents of the Ukrainian Helsinki Group*, 65–7.

70. *Memorandum no. 5:* "Ukraine of the Summer of 1977," 15 February 1977, *Documents of the Ukrainian Helsinki Group*, 74–6.

71. Ibid., 78–80.

72. See O. Berdnyk, "A Manifesto of the Ukrainian Human Rights Movement 1977," 9 November 1977, *Documents of the Ukrainian Helsinki Group*, 117–35; "The Positions of Ukrainian Political Prisoners: An Overview. A Joint Statement of Oleksa Tykhy and Father Vasyl Romanyuk," in Dobczansky, *Vasyl Romanyuk*, 107–17; I. Lytvyn, "Pravozakhysnyi rukh na

Ukraini, ioho zasady ta perspektyvy," *Suchasnist*, no. 10 (1979): 98–104. The Ukrainian Patriotic Movement issued at least four documents in the first part of 1980, including a call for decolonization of the USSR and independence for the nations within it, and an appeal in defence of Vladimir Klebanov (leader of an independent trade union group imprisoned in a psychiatric hospital), which urged Ukrainian workers to form independent trade unions. The identities of the authors of these documents were not revealed. See "Dokumenty Ukrainskoho patriotychnoho rukhu 1980 r.," *Visnyk represii v Ukraini*, no. 7 (1980).

73. See *Memorandum no. 7:* "The Ukrainian Group to Promote: The First Four Months," 15 March 1977, *Documents of the Ukrainian Helsinki Group*, 85–91.

74. A measure of the Ukrainian Helsinki monitors' early success in this respect is the fact that within four months of the group's inception, its members were able to claim that "hundreds of letters and complaints from all corners of Ukraine began to pour in to the members of the group as soon as people heard about its formation." See *Memorandum no. 7* (dated 15 March 1977), *Documents of the Ukrainian Helsinki Group*, 88.

Literary Politics and Literary Debates in Ukraine 1971–81

Myroslav Shkandrij

Toward the end of the sixties it was becoming clear that the relatively liberal party attitude toward literature which had characterized the decade was undergoing substantial modification.[1] The debate over Oles Honchar's *Sobor*, which appeared in January 1968,[2] was the first indication that stricter control of literature would be exercised in the future and less room allowed for nonconformist views.[3] The book's central idea, the seemingly innocuous affirmation of cultural continuity—especially with the Cossack past—was considered by some party officials symptomatic of everything ideologically "harmful, hostile to our reality."[4]

Honchar, nevertheless, remained the titular head of the Ukrainian Writers' Union until 1971, when he was replaced by another respected writer, Iurii Smolych. However, throughout this period it was the newly-promoted deputy head of the Union, Vasyl Kozachenko, who acted as the party's guardian of literary affairs and set the tone in literary debates.[5] At the Sixth Plenum of the Board of the Union of Writers of Ukraine in 1970, Kozachenko drew up a list of works which had deviated from the "correct ideological positions." Among the works criticized were Volodymyr Drozd's *Katastrofa*,[6] for its "overly morose atmosphere, full of helplessness, hopelessness"; Ivan Chendei's *Bereznevyi snih*,[7] for its "one-sided portrayal of the darker side of life in today's village of Zakarpattia, involuntarily deforming the true picture of collective farm reality"; Volodymyr Maniak's *Evrika*,[8] for "mocking the civic-patriotic ritual of life in a factory collective," for statements about "the levelling of the individual in our society," for "preaching dubious forms of behaviour," and for sympathizing with characters whose personalities are split, who are incorrigible and spiritually impoverished"; Roman Andriiashyk's *Poltva*,[9] whose book, Kozachenko claimed, portrayed events in Galicia after the

First World War in a manner different from that generally accepted in Marxist historiography, characterizing it as a work of "dubious historical value."[10] These comments by Kozachenko, the highest-ranking party figure in the Ukrainian Writers' Union and clearly the mouthpiece of party policy, were the signal for a concerted campaign against the books mentioned. In the years following the Sixth Plenum, the repeated and regular condemnation of these texts took on something of a ritualistic form and served as a warning to other writers.[11] To take only *Poltva* as an example, the book was again denounced at a special meeting of the Kiev writers' organization on 6 January 1971, lambasted several times in 1972, and attacked again in 1973 and 1974.[12]

At the same time as Kozachenko was setting stricter guidelines for writers in the Union, the campaign against Ivan Dziuba was drawing to a close. At first it had been demanded that Dziuba be stripped of his membership in the Writers' Union. Resistance to this step had been sufficient within the leadership of the Union to force a compromise: Dziuba remained a member but was compelled to sign a declaration, printed in *Literaturna Ukraina* on 6 January 1970, in which he renounced all links with "Ukrainian nationalism."[13]

The crushing of the movement for reform—Ivan Dziuba was a symbol of this movement—coincided with tougher official pronouncements concerning the national question. At the Twenty-fourth Congress of the Communist Party of the Soviet Union (CPSU), which met in Moscow from 30 March to 9 April 1971, Brezhnev asserted that the nationality issue had been resolved once and for all: a "single Soviet people" (*edinyi sovetskii narod*) had finally taken shape as a "historically new international community of people." The implication was that this was a transitional stage on the path to a single Soviet nation with Russian as a standard language. Ukrainian writers listening to this announcement must have reflected sadly upon the failure of the struggles of the preceding decade. Ever since 1961, when at the Twenty-second CPSU Congress Khrushchev stated that all Soviet nations and nationalities were "ever growing closer together" in a process of rapprochement (*sblizhenie*) which would lead eventually to a merger (*sliianie*), they had fought this policy, with its ominous implications for the Ukrainian language, literature and national identity. Now they had suffered another setback. After two brief "thaws" in the post-Stalin period in 1957–61 and 1966–68, were they once again to suffer a pogrom of Ukrainian culture?

The answer was not long in coming. At a meeting in Moscow on 30 December 1971, the Politburo decided to launch a concerted campaign against the dissident movement and *samvydav* publications.[14] Two weeks later, the arrests of hundreds of members of the Ukrainian intelligentsia began. The repercussions were felt in literary policy almost immediately.

On 21 January 1973, a resolution of the Central Committee of the CPSU, "On Literary-Artistic Criticism,"[15] demanded that critics be far more active in "implementing the party line in the area of artistic creativity." This resolution was the signal for renewed attacks upon "deviations" that had developed in previous years and a wide-ranging reassessment of much of the literature of the sixties.

Two other events at this time were important in shaping literary policy and creating the atmosphere in which writers were to work. The first was the fall of Petro Shelest, first secretary of the Communist Party of Ukraine, who was demoted and transferred to Moscow in May 1972. The second was Kozachenko's election as first secretary of the Ukrainian Writers' Union on 23 March 1973. His term of office, which lasted until 10 January 1979, was particularly repressive and marked by a continual search for ideological mistakes in the works of writers, and weaknesses in their world-view.

In April 1973 Shelest's book, *Ukraino nasha radianska*,[16] was attacked for a number of "ideological errors," "biased evaluations" of historical events and other "blunders" which were caused reportedly by his "local nationalism" and "national narrow-mindedness."[17] Critics were particularly indignant at Shelest's "idealization" of Ukraine's past and the way he dwelled on the country's distinctiveness, a violation of the "friendship of peoples" concept which demands that Ukraine's history be viewed as inseparable from—and usually subordinate to—Russian history.[18]

The distortions ascribed to Shelest, particularly his alleged glorification of the Zaporozhian Cossacks, were the alarm-signal for historical fiction. Similar distortions were immediately detected in works by Ivan Bilyk, Roman Ivanychuk, Iu. Kolisnychenko, S. Plachynda, R. Fedoriv and Ia. Stupak and the offending books removed from circulation.[19] Shelest had, in fact, complained publicly that "in our present-day historical and artistic literature, in motion pictures and the fine arts, the progressive role and significance of the Zaporozhian Sich, this glorious page in the heroic chronicle of the struggle of the Ukrainian people, have not been adequately depicted,"[20] and encouraged Ukrainian writers and artists to remedy the situation. After 1972, of course, the policy changed: the authorities criticized the portrayal of Ukrainian Cossack history in too glowing a light and discussion of the highly-sensitive problem of Ukrainian-Russian relations became dangerous for Ukrainian writers.

Several literary critics were at the same time criticized for twisting the party line. Among them were O. I. Karpenko for a study of Gogol, on the grounds that the latter figure was not to be taken seriously, since he idealized Cossack history;[21] V. Zaremba for a biography of the poet and folklorist, *Ivan Manzhura*;[22] I. Ilienko for another biography, *Hryhorii Kvitka-Osnovianenko*;[23] and M. Kytsenko for a study of Cossack legends and myths. *Voprosy istorii* attacked the last-named author for stressing only the negative aspects of the settlement of Ukrainian lands by Russians and for using the old term "foreign rabble" to refer to them.[24]

A good example of this almost pathological sensitivity toward the issue of Russian colonialism is the attack on Borys Kharchuk's "Dva dni"[25] by the critic H. Konovalov, who accused the author of openly besmirching "what we hold most sacred" in the following passage:

> In the hand-mill of any occupation—whether great-power Russian or great-power Polish—the snow-white ear of wheat was not produced, the flour was invariably black. The black flour of betrayal. And the invaders fed on it and continue to feed on it, grow, fat and vulgar, until the sword of new Bohuns flashes above their heads.[26]

Konovalov was affronted by the fact that Kharchuk wrote "with undisguised fury...about the reunification" of Ukraine and Russia in 1654. An insult to this cornerstone of Soviet nationalities policy—the ideas of "two brotherly peoples," of the essential identity of their cultures and destinies, and of their desire to live within one state structure—is detected by the reviewer in the following paragraph:

> The sturdy beeches, tall oaks were green with spreading branches at the bottom and were drying up at the top. They had seen enough of winged dragoons, grey-coated guardsmen, heard all sorts of cannons from various sides and also the different languages of tribes that became people and attempted to seize for themselves, to place under their liberating guardianship, the land from which those beeches and oaks grow.[27]

The reviewer also takes offence at the following monologue by the lawyer, Huslysty, who has agreed to defend his former teacher, a Communist, and peasants at a trial in prewar Poland:

> Every political trial, even the smallest, is historical. And it begins on that first, distant day, when the first conquerors set foot on our soil. The judges will change, so will the accused, but the trial will continue until the last conqueror lies dead. Justice—is freedom.... The oppression of one person is the oppression of an entire people. To deprive even one person of the right to think and to take away his freedom is to rob the intelligence and freedom of an entire society.[28]

On the basis of this passage the critic accused Kharchuk of "abstract humanism" and an "trans-social and trans-historical approach" to life.[29] A fierce barrage of attacks was mounted against Kharchuk at the end of 1973 and the early months of 1974.[30] Eventually he admitted his mistakes and attacked "the camp of Ukrainian bourgeois nationalism abroad" for "kicking up a storm" about his case.[31]

It was not only historical writing that was put on the carpet during Kozachenko's term of office. The party expressed profound dissatisfaction with the entire critical establishment for complacency and lack of vigilance. *Radianska Ukraina* had set the tone in 1972 by declaring that "the state of affairs in Ukrainian criticism does not fulfill demands made by the party." In the same article, it chided *Literaturna Ukraina* and *Vitchyzna* for the poverty of their literary criticism, denounced "subjectivism" in assessing literary affairs and criticized the eighth volume of the *History of Ukrainian Literature*.[32] Although it has since been suggested that sections of this history—one of the many scholarly achievements of the sixties—be rewritten, no revised editions have as yet appeared and the proposal seems to have been dropped.[33]

Once the party had given the signal, ideological experts within the Writers' Union began to sift through the literature of the last decade. The names of arrested oppositionists, such as Ie. Sverstiuk, I. Svitlychny and M. Osadchy, simply disappeared from literary affairs: their names have not appeared in print since 1971. Other authors were told to mend their ways, and individual works by them were faulted. Vitalii Korotych's *Perevtilennia* was found lacking because of poems dealing with such "trans-class categories as conscience, good and evil in general,"[34] Iryna Zhylenko's *Avtoportret u chervonomu* for a "narrow-minded view of the world,"[35] D. Mishchenko's *V mori zatyshku nemaie* for "deheroization,"[36] and various works of Ievhen Hutsalo for glorifying "the modern, 'intellectual'...philistine,"[37] for using "the stream of consciousness technique...modelled on Western examples,"[38] for "portraying parodies of the Soviet people," while failing to show the role of the party and Komsomol organizations in the life of the collective farm," and a host of other sins.[39]

Kozachenko used his election as first secretary of the Ukrainian Writers' Union at the Fourth Plenum of the Board, on 23 March 1973, to launch a tirade against writers who had fallen under the influence of "bourgeois nationalism." Among writers singled out were Oles Berdnyk, Ivan Bilyk, Roman Andriiashyk and the two translators, M. Lukash and Hryhorii Kochur.[40] He accused the latter of subscribing to the views of the neo-classicist poet and scholar Mykola Zerov, who disappeared during the purges and whose views on literature and cultural policy have always been considered a dangerous form of "bourgeois nationalism": Zerov demanded a knowledge of the best in European literature and encouraged the study of the classical heritage. The translations from the European classics by Kochur and Lukash were criticized precisely for their sophistication. It was charged that under the pretext of enriching the language they were introducing archaisms and were attempting "to squeeze the living language out of literature, especially where it was naturally and logically related to

Russian." If, asserted the critics, such tendencies continue, "we would have a dead literary language, a Ukrainian Latin." It is, of course, an axiom of linguistic policy that, wherever parallelisms exist, the use of the Russian word is both more natural and logical. "Besides all this," concluded the critics, "such a vocabulary repels the reader by its intentional refinement, its strained 'intellectualism' and, above all, clouds the essence of the matter.... In short, in literary criticism as in everything else we require 'a maximum of Marxism—a maximum of the popular and simple'."[41]

The critics also attacked the introduction of religious themes in literature. Mykola Rudenko's *Vsesvit u tobi*, (1968) and M. Medunytsia's story "Voskovi olivtsi" were condemned on this ground by L. Sanov, as was Oles Berdnyk's *Zorianyi korsar* (1971).[42] These charges were followed by disciplinary action against selected writers. Several were thrown out of the Writers' Union—among them O. Berdnyk, H. Kochur and M. Lukash—while the work of others was placed on the index and removed from public libraries.[43]

This kind of pressure achieved its goal of intimidating writers, some of whom ceased writing while others attempted to bend toward the new party line. A good example of the latter is Ievhen Hutsalo, one of the most talented prose writers of the preceding decade. Capitulating to party demands, he produced together with Rostyslav Sambuk, a "made-to-order" work of propagandistic journalism, "Stepova Rodyna".[44] The book was evidently an attempt to give Caesar his due. It was a response to Kozachenko's demands at the Fourth Plenum in March 1973, which had stated that the party required not intimate personal lyrics but songs which could be useful in inspiring collective farm brigades and factory workers; that in prose, priority be given to journalistic sketches; and that the new emphasis in party propaganda was upon Soviet multinationalism, upon the "mutual links" and "mutual interaction" of Soviet peoples and their literatures.[45] Hutsalo and Sambuk responded to the new turn in the party line by producing a report on the village of Sursko-Mykhailivka, in which they proudly asserted the co-existence of a variety of nationalities that worked together cheerfully and co-operatively. This kind of literary exercise, written in a style that was a radical departure from that used in other works by the writers, was, as one might expect, an artistic failure. The two authors, consequently, were criticized for writing in an "exceedingly colourless and ... unnatural" manner.[46] A similar metamorphosis was attempted by other writers of stature, in an attempt to adapt to the demands of party authorities.[47] Needless to say, they were invariably poorly received by both critics and reading public.

In 1974 the literary authorities began to correct some alleged mistaken evaluations of the classics of Ukrainian literature. They suggested that Ivan Franko was being idealized by some literary critics who found that his views on literary criticism were more sensitive and far less dogmatic than those of N. Dobroliubov and A. Chernyshevsky. The authorities interpreted this as a veiled attack on dogmatism in contemporary literary criticism, and reminded the offending author that "the great socialists, Chernyshevsky and Dobroliubov, were the highest achievement of the leading literary-critical thought of their time" and that "Ivan Franko was a convinced representative of that school during a later period."[48] They also criticized a tendency to overestimate the work of Panteleimon Kulish and his impact upon Ukrainian intellectual history.[49] Certain critics, they declared, in praising and popularizing the work of VAPLITE,[50] were rehabilitating the organization itself,[51] and certain authors, in juxtaposing the 1920s in the history of Soviet literature with the 1930s, were "whitewashing VAPLITE and blackening VUSPP, representing Khvyliovism as a 'constructive' current in Soviet literature."[52] Clearly, in all three cases the guardians of orthodoxy were particularly worried by the possible appearance of a competing literary theory or programme for a "new direction" in criticism. Such a course would obviously begin with a reappraisal of the classics of Ukrainian literary criticism.

In spite of the threats and cajolery, the situation in creative literature and literary criticism remained far from satisfactory from the party's point of view. There were repeated attacks on the incompetence and indolence of critics: of 114 critics in the Writers' Union, "only 10-15 worked actively in literature," complained Zahrebelny in 1978. The rest maintained a watchful restraint or simply kept silent. As for literature itself, Zahrebelny characterized it as "one-dimensional":

> All the features of a novel are there, heroes, conflict, *sujet*, plot, *dénouement*, dialogues, scenery, comment by the author, information, everything just as it should be, and yet everything is dead, unnatural, repetitive, a fake and not the original unique creation.[53]

The opening up of this kind of discussion is not new to Soviet literature; the same complaints, often couched in exactly the same language have been voiced periodically since the twenties. At the basis of the discussion is the problem of defining literature and socialist realism. If the party insists on reducing all literature to propaganda, on viewing it as part of the campaign of psychological warfare with the West, or the manufacturing of socialist realist "archetypes" which presents members of the *nomenklatura* in a suitable light, then there will be a continual conflict between the party's demands upon writers and the concept of literature which, whether they admit to it or not, is held by the vast majority of writers in the Soviet Union. For the party demands that writers portray life as it ought to be and describe the situation as the government would like to see it develop. In other words, there is a tendency to start with an ideal image and to fit the reality to it. When the standard images are distorted, the propaganda experts are quick to detect this and the process of browbeating the writers, of demanding that they "rebuild" themselves begins.

Writers in the Soviet Union have, on the other hand, consistently demonstrated that they adhere to a different definition of literature and see the social role of literature in terms that conflict with the party line. The last major assault on the party's reduction of literature to an illustration of official resolutions was mounted during the de-Stalinization period. It became clear that the new generation of critics—Ivan Svitlychny, Ivan Dziuba, Ievhen Sverstiuk, Ivan Boychak and others—did not consider this kind of caressing of the readers by repeating stock situations and wish-fulfillment images as literature at all. They argued, in the tradition of the critical realists of the nineteenth century, that literature should play a leading role in social criticism, that it should be exploring new and uncharted territories and that it could only achieve the stature of greatness if it was completely honest, and able to dig beneath the everyday surface phenomena of life to the deeper problems that lay beneath.

It was this new concept of literature that the party was determined to crush in the campaign that began around 1968. It is, however, clear that this campaign shattered the dreams for a new world and a new literature that many, perhaps most of the new generation, cherished at the end of the fifties and the beginning of the sixties, and that it clipped the wings of the vast majority of talented writers who came upon the scene during the years of hope that followed Khrushchev's speech at the Twentieth CPSU Congress. As a result, not only did the creative work of individual writers suffer, but entire genres began to atrophy.

On 10 January 1979, Kozachenko was removed from the leadership of the Writers' Union and replaced by Pavlo Zahrebelny. Dissatisfaction with Kozachenko's regime must have reached a very high level at this time because many writers seem to have simply retreated into a shell. When, for example, Zahrebelny sent out a questionnaire concerning the crisis in the novel, only 10 persons out of 150 even bothered to write back.[54] As a consequence, the new head initiated a campaign against the state of Ukrainian literary affairs; it was suddenly discovered that there was a crisis in sector after sector: publishing, the novel, drama, theatre, the novella, literary theory, the ethics of criticism. The voicing of these complaints began an officially-sanctioned "literary discussion" in order to air some of the grievances that had accumulated in the previous six years.

At the same time a resolution of the CPSU, "On the Further Improvement of Ideological, Political-Educational Work," issued on 26 April 1979, also drew attention to the unsatisfactory nature of much that had passed for literature or criticism and to the discontent of an increasingly sophisticated readership, thus further encouraging the flow of complaints.

Borys Oliinyk spoke of the "necessity of creating a moral-ethical creative atmosphere" that would be conducive to the production of quality literature, and thus implied that such an atmosphere had not existed in the past.[55] The Soviet press scolded writers for "fearing to put before the general public topical problems of our social life."[56] It admitted that nothing at all was known about the reader; no attempt had been made to study the sociology of taste. Only the fact that thousands of copies of books highly acclaimed by the party remained unsold indicated the passive resistance of the reader to some works. The authorities fiercely attacked the critics and reminded them that their inertia was creating a vacuum which could lead to the loss of the youth. Zahrebelny complained that the critics specializing in foreign literature seemed to enjoy reading Kafka and Vonnegut so much that they had not found time to say a word about Ukrainian literature.[57]

Various aspects of the relationship between the writer and publisher were discussed at this time as younger writers complained of having their work vetted and changed arbitrarily by publishers, or that it took an average of four to five years to get a book into print. But the most significant problem, which has been alluded to recently several times—albeit in somewhat muffled tones—was the "difficulty with paper."[58] It is an unspoken fact that since 1972 the number of titles and the volume of Ukrainian books published in the republic has fallen, while the corresponding figure for Russian books has jumped significantly. The "difficulty with paper" obviously affects Ukrainian publications alone and is part of party policy. By the end of the decade the ratio of Russian to Ukrainian titles produced in the republic was approaching three to one (see Table 1). Ironically the number of Ukrainian titles produced at this time fell behind the number that had been produced in the mid-twenties, before the Ukrainianization policy began in earnest.[59]

The "difficulty with paper" phenomenon is not new. Nervous publishers do not always find it easy to reject a work that is written by a famous writer, or one in which specific ideological errors cannot be detected. Sometimes the party line on a certain author, or a certain described event, may be unclear or in process of change. Rather than take a risk, a careful editor will often invoke the old standby: there is no paper. It has been claimed by at least one Soviet literary historian[60] that, during the period we are examining, up to 80 per cent of submitted manuscripts were denied publication on the grounds of a paper shortage. Ukrainian book publishing has been deteriorating steadily since the sixties. A quick glance at UNESCO statistics shows that in 1979, of the ten largest Slavic-speaking peoples, Ukrainian occupied seventh place according to the number of book titles published. This number was only slightly more than that produced by the Slovenes, a nation of under two millions (see Table 2).

TABLE 1 Books Published in Ukraine 1970-9

	Total no. of titles published in Ukraine	No. of titles published in per cent	
		In Ukrainian	In Russian
1970	8,133	38.2	37.6
1971	8,068	38.5	57.2
1972	9,407	36.9	58.4
1973	7,686	38.8	57.4
1974	8,814	32.8	63.1
1975	8,731	30.4	65.2
1976	9,110	27.4	68.6
1977	8,430	28.1	67.9
1978	8,259	27.7	68.2
1979	9,032	26.7	69.6

SOURCE: *Pechat SSSR v 1970 godu* (Moscow 1971).

The effect of Soviet cultural policy on Ukrainian book production can be grasped by making a comparison with the number of titles published with the number of language speakers among the ten largest Slavic-language groups. It becomes immediately clear that the two Slavic nations within the Soviet Union, the Ukrainians and Belorussians, fare very poorly as compared to the Southern and Western Slavs (see Table 3). Since 1970 the situation has deteriorated still further. For an estimated population of 36.4 million Ukrainian language speakers[61] in 1979, the 2,414 titles produced in Ukraine in that year constitute only 66.3 titles per million speakers.

The discussion in the press, which began in the late 1970s and is still continuing, contains many candid statements about the problems facing Ukrainian literature. On the question of Ukrainian drama, for instance, press items pointed out that for a population of some 50 millions, there were only three or four dramatists,[62] that the years 1976-9 had not produced a single play of any merit,[63] that the Ukrainian plays accounted for only a quarter of the republic's repertoire in 1978, that the majority of the plays which had runs of over 100 performances were pre-revolutionary classics and that much of the contemporary production was "trash."[64] The press also noted that the last tragedy to have appeared was O. Levada's *Faust i smert* in 1960, that satire was no longer being produced, and that theatres were afraid of putting on comedies or political plays with any contemporary themes.[65] Pondering the reasons for this deplorable state of affairs, one critic ingenuously suggested that it had something to do with the "timidity of some authors and theatres toward making use of the sharp

TABLE 2 Slavic-Language Book Titles, 1964–78

Language	No. of titles published in native languages by each country														
	1964	1965	1966	1967	1968	1969	1970	1971	1972	1973	1974	1975	1976	1977	1978
Russian	56,391	57,521	54,968	56,225	57,522	57,072	60,240	65,055	61,239	61,856		60,259	66,126	66,180	
Polish	7,457	7,238	8,136	8,721	8,437	8,571	9,271	9,462	9,799	9,562	8,857	9,543	10,503	10,563	10,900
Serbo-Croat	5,492	5,516	5,507	6,187	6,474	5,728	5,402	6,541	6,448	6,353	8,220	7,492	5,939	7,042	7,102
Czech[a]	4,159	4,692	4,577	4,383	4,528		5,067	5,230	5,735	5,318	5,498	6,520	6,144	5,895	6,042
Bulgarian		3,236	3,021	3,301	3,117	3,144	3,368	3,640	3,433	3,565	3,422	3,201	3,204	3,496	3,671
Ukrainian		3,003	3,026	2,855	2,950	3,061	3,112	3,113	3,414	2,989	2,893	2,651	2,494	2,367	2,287
Slovak[a]	3,173	3,119	2,611	2,470	2,446		2,804	2,623	2,842	2,232	3,311	2,875	2,495	2,829	2,739
Slovenian	1,773	985	945	1,236	1,139	1,152	1,089	1,365	1,463	1,515	2,444	1,773	1,594	1,630	1,838
Macedonian	403	425	387	596	574	532	618	748	652	726	789	760	559	490	480
Belorussian	339	299	336	344	453	425	430	423	405	467	439	476	476	393	373

SOURCE: *UNESCO Statistical Yearbook* (Paris 1964–).

[a] A small number of bilingual Czech-Slovak editions have been excluded.

TABLE 3 **Number of titles published compared to number of language speakers in 1970**[63]

Language	Speakers (millions)	Titles	Titles per million speakers
Russian	141.0	60,240	427.2
Ukrainian	35.0	3,112	88.9
Polish	32.0	9,271	289.4
Serbo-Croat	15.1	5,271	357.7
Czech	9.5	5,067	533.3
Bulgarian	7.6	3,368	443.1
Belorussian	7.3	430	58.9
Slovak	4.0	2,804	701.0
Slovenian	1.8	1,089	605.0
Macedonian	1.0	618	618.0

SOURCE: B. Struminsky, "Sotsiolingvistychna pozytsiia ukrainstva v slovianskii hrupi mov," *Ukrainska knyha* 7, no. 4 (1977): 86.

weapon of satire and humour" because they were constantly glancing over their shoulder out of fear that "someone would misunderstand them or take offence, or perhaps even recognize himself and take the laughter as directed at his institution or person."[66]

Perhaps the two most interesting aspects of the officially encouraged "literary discussion" of 1980-1 were the parallel debates on style and ethics. The first saw a number of critics discuss the merits of various stylistic tendencies. Some conservative writers and critics expressed a deep suspicion of new "isms," of structural complexity and stylistic innovation. They were challenged by younger authors who defended experimental prose, psychologism and the "mythological-folkloric" trend.[67] The discussion evidently ended in a compromise, with calls for the recognition of the merits of each approach.

The second aspect of the "literary discussion," the debate on ethics, was much more bitter. The barbs in this debate were aimed at the all-powerful hack who passes off his personal prejudices as critical judgments. Generally, the discussants charged, such a critic applies a crude sociological analysis to a work of art, assuming for some reason that the writer's method is exactly the same as his. If his method does not work, however, he asserts that the book is a poor one and unworthy of serious consideration. The debate raised some much deeper problems about the nature of socialist realism and the kind of critical approaches that could be taken toward a work. It quickly became clear that there was no agreement about the question of critical method and the discussion again ended on a conciliatory note.[68]

This most recent "literary discussion" is considered to have begun with H. Shtol's article in *Literaturna Ukraina* on 2 December 1980 and V. Maniak's item in the same newspaper on 5 December 1980. It ended inconclusively with a series of articles in *Literaturna Ukraina* on 3 April 1981. The attempt to stage this kind of open critique of literary problems may be part of a conciliatory policy toward the Ukrainian intelligentsia by the party. Possibly the havoc wreaked by the arrests and the hounding of writers during Kozachenko's period in office evoked a strong reaction within the literary and artistic intelligentsia, and the party, in turn, decided to ease some of the restrictions in literary and cultural policy. The removal of Vitalii Vinohradsky as editor of *Literaturna Ukraina* in March 1980 and the nomination of Lina Kostenko for the Shevchenko State Prize in Literature in December 1980 may be part of such a policy of relaxation. Lina Kostenko was a leading figure among the literary generation of the sixties and had been silent for over a decade. Recently, three books by her appeared in print: *Nad berehamy vichnoi riky* (1977), *Marusia Churai* (1979) and *Nepovtornist* (1980). A very favourable review of the acclaimed *Marusia Churai* appeared under Mykola Bazhan's name in *Literaturna Ukraina* on 4 March 1980, perhaps signalling a change in attitude toward the poetess on the part of the authorities. To these signs of improvement in the literary climate might be added the publication of L. Kyselov's talented and rather bold second abridged collection of poetry *Ostannia pisnia* (1979), which was heavily censored in 1970, and the appearance of V. Symonenko's collection *Lebedi materynstva* (1981).[69]

On the other hand, this may signify nothing more than the party's flirtation with public opinion, a correcting and smoothing over of its own mistakes. The party's control of literary affairs seems to be total, and no substantial deviation from its policy of provincializing Ukrainian literature can be detected. Quite the contrary; D. Pavlychko may have been removed from his position as editor-in-chief of *Vsesvit*, an important publication that translates foreign authors into Ukrainian, precisely because of the above-average standards of this journal. His successor, Vitalii Korotych, has stated that he intends to change the journal's format to that of the American *Reader's Digest*. In addition, the unrelenting attacks on any expressions of Ukrainian patriotism have continued with R. Bratun's removal as chairman of the Lviv branch of the Writer's Union for his speech at the funeral of Volodymyr Ivasiuk, a young composer, who, it is generally assumed, was murdered by the KGB in May 1979. It should also be stated that this "discussion" is but a pale reflection of the two preceding "thaws" which covered the same ground in more outspoken terms.

It may also be that the party authorities are concerned about the attitudes of the younger generation of writers and critics, whose tastes and attitudes differ from those of the old guard and who draw their inspiration from the best of the sixties, and not from the turgid products often served up as models today. Considerable stress has recently been placed upon the need to "educate" these younger members of the intelligentsia and a number of special schools and seminars have been organized to accelerate this grooming process.

Whether such a policy of relaxation is indeed being attempted, and what its effects will be, remain to be seen. The results of the policy of the seventies, however, are evident: it succeeded in suppressing nonconformist attitudes and disciplining the intelligentsia. Perhaps V. Shcherbytsky pronounced the best epitaph on the decade when he reviewed its achievements at the Eighth Conference of the Ukrainian Writers' Union in April 1981:

> There was a time when the Ukrainian Writers' Union and the party organizations conducted unavoidable educational work with individual literary figures who had committed mistakes. And today their talent honestly serves the people![70]

It remains to be seen whether the "educational work" currently being conducted on the next generation of the Ukrainian intelligentsia will succeed in eradicating similar nonconformist tendencies.

Notes

1. For critical surveys of Ukrainian literature during this period, see G. S. N. Luckyj, "The Ukrainian Literary Scene Today," *Slavic Review* 31 (December 1972): 863–9, and "Ukrainian Literature," in G. S. N. Luckyj, ed., *Discordant Voices: The Non-Russian Soviet Literatures, 1953–1973* (Oakville 1975); I. Koshelivets, *Suchasna literatura v URSR* (New York 1964); "Pieciolatki literatury ukraińskiej," *Kultura* (September, 1971): 64–74; and "Literatura 1978," *Suchasnist*, no. 3 (1979): 145–58; Ia. Pelenski, "Recent Ukrainian Writing," *Survey*, no. 4 (1966): 102–12; A. de Vicenz, "Recent Ukrainian Writing," *Survey*, no. 1 (1963): 143–50. For anthologies of the literature of the "thaw" in Ukraine, see I. Koshelivets, ed., *Panorama nainovishoi literatury v URSR: poeziia, proza, krytyka*, 2d ed., rev. and enl. (Munich 1974); B. Kravtsiv, *Shistdesiat poetiv shistdesiatykh rokiv: antolohiia ukrainskoi poezii* (New York 1967); and *Soviet Literature*, no. 5 (1973), which is devoted entirely to Ukrainian literature.

2. The novel first appeared in the journal *Vitchyzna* (January 1968). Both Dnipro (Kiev 1968) and Radianskyi pysmennyk (Kiev 1968) publishers put the novel out in book form. The first volume of the planned *Collected Works* of Honchar appeared in 1978 with a list of contents of subsequent volumes; *Sobor*, however, is not among them.

3. The literature on *Sobor* is substantial. For the more important articles on this book, see Ie. Sverstiuk, *Sobor u ryshtovanni* (Paris-Baltimore 1970); "Lyst tvorchoi molodi Dnipropetrovska," *Suchasnist*, no. 2 (1969): 75–85; *Ukrainskyi visnyk* (Paris-Baltimore 1970), 1: 39–50.

4. The words belong to the head of the ideological section of the Dnipropetrovsk oblast committee of the party, and are quoted in *Molod Dnipropetrovska v borotbi proty rusyfikatsii* (New York 1971), 10.

5. Kozachenko was well-trusted in party circles. He was elected a candidate member of the Central Committee of the Communist Party of Ukraine at its Twenty-third Congress (1966), and a member of the Central Committee at the party's Twenty-fourth (1971) and Twenty-fifth (1976) congresses. He also served as a deputy to both the USSR and the Ukrainian Supreme Soviet. He was the author of an attack on Ivan Svitlychny four months before the latter's arrest ("Tobi, narode!" in *Literaturna Ukraina*, 27 April 1965), and seems to have been assigned the task of reproving those writers who had signed the famed appeal by 139 citizens of Kiev protesting the trials then taking place (see his article in *Literaturna Ukraina*, 21 May 1968). The case of the appeal is documented in M. Browne, ed., *Ferment in the Ukraine* (London 1971), 23, 24, 197.

6. *Katastrofa* appeared in *Vitchyzna*, no. 2 (1968). It was reprinted in *Suchasnist*, no. 1–3 (1969).

7. *Bereznevyi snih*, published in Kiev in 1968, was criticized in an article entitled "Diisnist i pozytsiia pysmennyka" which appeared in *Zakarpatska pravda*, 18 July 1969. According to a report in *Ukrainskyi visnyk* 1–2, 215–16, the author was expelled from the party and from leadership of the writers' organization of Zakarpattia.

8. This first appeared in the journal *Dnipro*, no. 2 (1967).

9. The book first appeared in the journal *Prapor*, no. 8 and 9 (1969); it was reprinted in *Suchasnist*, no. 2–5 (1971). Part three of *Poltva* never appeared, although its publication was promised in *Prapor*, no. 8 (1969).

10. V. Kozachenko's speech at the Sixth Plenum of the Ukrainian Writers' Union was reprinted in *Literaturna Ukraina*, 20 November 1970, under the title "Budivnyk komunizmu—heroi suchasnoi literatury."

11. See V. Svoboda, "Partiine kerivnytstvo literaturoiu v Ukraini: persha polovyna simdesiatykh rokiv," *Vitrazh*, no. 10–11 (1980), which contains much interesting information on the literary scandals of this period and to which this paper is indebted.

12. For attacks on *Poltva*, see B. Dudykevych in *Radianska Ukraina*, 8 December 1970 (his article was reprinted in *Suchasnist*, no. 2 (1971): 8–12); and "Vsuperech istorychnii pravdi," *Literaturna Ukraina*, 12 January 1971; and I. Doroshenko, "A z pozytsii realizmu? Shche pro roman R. Andriiashyka *Poltva*," *Literaturna Ukraina*, 26 January 1961.

13. I. Dziuba, "Zaiava do prezydii SPU," *Literaturna Ukraina*, 6 January 1970.

14. The Politburo meeting is mentioned in *Ukrainskyi visnyk* 7–8, 124–5.

15. See *Literaturna Ukraina*, 28 January 1972.

16. P. Iu. Shelest, *Ukraino, nasha radianska* (Kiev 1970).
17. "Pro seriozni nedoliky ta pomylky odniei knyhy," *Komunist Ukrainy*, no. 4 (1973): 77–82.
18. For a discussion of Shelest's book and the implications of his fall for Ukrainian historians, see L. Tillet, "Ukrainian Nationalism and the Fall of Shelest," *Slavic Review*, no. 4 (1973): 752–68.
19. I. Bilyk was attacked for *Mech Areia* (Kiev 1972); R. Ivanychuk for *Malvy* (Kiev 1968); Iu. Kolisnychenko and S. Plachynda for *Neopalyma kupyna* (Kiev 1968); Ia. Stupak for "Hordynia," *Vitchyzna*, no. 12 (1966). See also M. Z. Shamota's attacks in "Za konkretno-istorychne vidobrazhennia zhyttia v literaturi," *Komunist Ukrainy* (May 1973).
20. Shelest, *Ukraino nasha radianska*, 22.
21. See *Literaturna Ukraina*, 20 July 1973.
22. V. Zaremba's *Ivan Manzhura* (Kiev 1972). The author was attacked for underemphasizing the class struggle and for ignoring the evils of hetman rule. One reviewer wrote: "What purpose does Zaremba's lack of objectivity serve? Is its aim to show that the misfortunes and troubles suffered by Ukraine were brought by others, rather than its own feudal Ukrainian lords?" *Raduga*, no. 6 (1973); translated by *Digest of Soviet Ukrainian Press*, no. 12 (1973): 15–17.
23. I. Ilienko, *Hryhorii Kvitka-Osnovianenko* (Kiev 1973).
24. M. Kytsenko's *Khortytsia v heroitsi i lehendakh*, 2d ed. (Dnipropetrovsk 1972) was attacked in E. I. Druzhinina's "Po povodu odnoi broshury," *Voprosy istorii*, no. 11 (1972): 203–5.
25. B. Kharchuk, "Dva dni" appeared in his *Materynska liubov* (Kiev 1972).
26. H. Konovalov, "Antyistorychni vpravy B. Kharchuka," *Literaturna Ukraina*, 18 December 1973.
27. Ibid.
28. Ibid.
29. Ibid.
30. For attacks on Kharchuk, see *Literaturna Ukraina*, 18 September 1973; 7 December 1973; 18 December 1973; 28 December 1973; 1 March 1974; and 22 March 1974. The whole Kharchuk episode is analysed in *Svoboda*, "Partiine kerivnytstvo."
31. "Vidpovid panakhydnykam," *Literaturna Ukraina*, 28 June 1974.
32. For the attacks, see *Radianska Ukraina*, 29 January 1972. The eighth volume of *Istoriia ukrainskoi literatury* was published by the Academy of Sciences of the Ukrainian SSR (Kiev 1972).
33. The suggestion was made by L. Novychenko concerning the eighth volume (*Literaturna Ukraina*, 4 February 1972) and by O. Kylymnyk concerning the sixth volume, which deals with the 1920s and 1930s (*Literaturna Ukraina*, 29 January 1974).
34. *Perevtilennia* (Kiev 1972) was attacked by Iu. Zbanatsky in *Literaturna Ukraina*, 8 February 1972.
35. *Avtoportret u chervonomu* (Kiev 1971) was also attacked by Zbanatsky (ibid.)

36. Mishchenko's book (Kiev 1970) was criticized by P. Zahrebelny in *Literaturna Ukraina*, 20 May 1971.

37. This was an attack on "Dvoie na sviati kokhannia," *Vitchyzna*, no. 6 (1973) by the critic L. Sanov in *Literaturna Ukraina*, 7 August 1973.

38. An attack on the same work by M. Shamota in *Literaturna Ukraina*, 19 April 1974.

39. An attack on "Teche richka" and *Berezhanski portrety* (Kiev 1975) by M. Lohvynenko in *Radianska Ukraina*, 27 July 1975. He was also attacked by Iu. Zbanatsky for *Mertva zona* (Kiev 1967) in *Literaturna Ukraina*, 3 March 1972; and by B. Chaly in *Literaturna Ukraina*, 7 December 1973.

40. *Literaturna Ukraina*, 27 March 1973.

41. These comments were made by M. Shamota in "Pytannia suchasnoho literaturoznavstva," *Radianske literaturoznavstvo*, no. 3 (1974): 52.

42. For L. Sanov's comments, see *Radianske literaturoznavstvo*, no. 16 (1974): 23–6; and for comments on Berdnyk, see M. Lohvynenko's attack in *Literaturna Ukraina*, 11 August 1972. Berdnyk was also attacked in *Literaturna Ukraina* on 21 April 1972 for "preachings filled with Biblical, Buddhist and Yogic dogmas, as well as maxims of various charlatans.... " and again in *Literaturna Ukraina* on 27 March and 15 May 1973.

43. See *Ukrainskyi visnyk* 7–8, 123–4.

44. Appeared in *Vitchyzna*, no. 12 (1975).

45. For information on recent trends in nationality policy and how this affects literature, see Luckyj, "Socialist in Content and National In Form," in his *Discordant Voices: The Non-Russian Soviet Literatures*, 1–12.

46. See *Literaturna Ukraina*, 12 December 1975.

47. See, for example, V. Drozd's "Liudy na zemli" in *Vitchyzna*, no. 7 (1975). The phenomenon is a familiar one in the political arena: Ivan Dziuba bought his freedom by putting his name to *Hrani krystala*, (Kiev 1975) which purported to refute his powerful *Internationalism or Russification?* (New York 1974).

48. See M. Z. Shamota, "Pytannia suchasnoho literaturoznavstva," *Radianske literaturoznavstvo*, no. 3 (1974): 45–6. A second attack on the idealization of Franko appeared in P. Io. Kolesnyk, "Literaturoznavchi aberatsii," *Radianske literaturoznavstvo*, no. 5 (1974): 57–9.

49. See Kolesnyk, "Literaturoznavchi aberatsii," 55–6.

50. VAPLITE (Vilna Akademiia proletarskoi literatury—Free Academy of Proletarian Literature) was an organization formed in the mid-twenties by Mykola Khvyliovy and other prominent revolutionary writers and acted as the main competitor and opposition to the party-sponsored VUSPP. VAPLITE was accused of "bourgeois nationalism" and a "Western-European orientation."

51. Kolesnyk, "Literaturoznavchi aberatsii," 56.

52. Shamota, "Pytannia suchasnoho literaturoznavstva," 55.

53. P. Zahrebelny, "Obrii romanu," *Radianske literaturoznavstvo*, no. 7 (1978): 24.

54. Ibid., 9.
55. See *Radianske literaturoznavstvo*, no. 9 (1979): 81.
56. See *Literaturna Ukraina*, 22 June 1979.
57. See P. Zahrebelny's speech in *Literaturna Ukraina*, 9 April 1981, and Novychenko's in ibid., 14 April 1981.
58. See Zahrebelny's speech in *Literaturna Ukraina*, 9 April 1981.
59. See V. Sukhyno-Khomenko, " Piatyrichka ukrainskoi radianskoi knyzhky," *Krytyka*, no. 10–11 (1929): 11.
60. G. Svirski, *A History of Post-War Soviet Writing* (Ann Arbor 1981), 345.
61. *Naselenie SSSR po dannym vsesoiuznoi perepisi naseleniia 1979 goda* (Moscow 1980), 28.
62. See V. Boyko in *Literaturna Ukraina*, 26 January 1979.
63. O. Kolomiiets, "Ukrainska dramaturhiia sohodni," *Radianske literaturoznavstvo*, no. 11 (1979): 6.
64. Among the twenty-two most popular plays of 1978 were classics by H. Kvitka-Osnovianenko, I. Karpenko-Kary, I. Kotliarevsky and M. Starytsky, as well as plays based on works by Gogol and Shevchenko. (Ibid., 10.)
65. See *Literaturna Ukraina*, 17 March 1981.
66. See "Buty hidnym svoho poklykannia," ibid., 20 April 1979.
67. Contributors to this discussion include: P. Zahrebelny and O. Levada in ibid., 11 April 1980; V. Maniak in ibid., 5 December 1980; A. Pohribny, in ibid., 6 January 1981; V. Dobriansky in ibid., 13 January 1981; V. Iavorisky in *Dnipro*, no. 1 (1980): 146–9; K. Lomazova in *Literaturna Ukraina*, 3 February 1981; A. Kolisnychenko in ibid., 20 March 1981; V. Koval in ibid., 16 January 1981; "Po kolu chy po spirali?" in ibid., 24 March 1981; and Iu. Vynnychuk, "Ryfy styliu," ibid., 3 April 1981.
68. Among contributors were H. Shtol in *Literaturna Ukraina*, 2 December 1980; M. Slavynsky in ibid., 16 December 1980; M. Slaboshpytsky in ibid., 3 April 1981; and Iu. Burliai's "Literaturna krytyka, ii metod," *Radianske literaturoznavstvo*, no. 6 (1980): 62–73.
69. I am indebted here and in the comments that follow to Professor Jaroslav Rozumny of the University of Manitoba who was kind enough to read and comment on this paper.
70. *Literaturna Ukraina*, 9 April 1981.

The Ukrainian Economy in the 1970s

Gennady Ozornoy

In 1971, Ukraine started its Ninth Five-Year Plan. At this time it was faced with new constraints on its economic growth. Throughout the 1960s, Ukraine had depleted those reserves that had sustained rapid industrial development in the past. In that decade Ukraine's economic growth owed much to the expansion of the labour force, high rates of capital investment and the importation of new technology from the West. Around 1970, having depleted its labour reserves, the Ukrainian economy could no longer develop through this extensive mode. Between 1950 and 1970, the average annual rate of increase of both civilian non-agricultural and industrial employment was 4.7 per cent. Between 1971 and 1980, on the other hand, the average annual rate of increase was only 1.8 and 1.3 per cent respectively.[1] The prospects for the 1980s are even less encouraging since an unusually small number of young people will be entering the labour force.

If high rates of economic development were to be continued in the 1970s—and this was imperative if the economy was to meet rising consumer expectations and pressing claims from other economic sectors—then it was necessary to compensate for the levelling off of non-agricultural employment by raising significantly the growth rate of capital stock. Had it been introduced, this rate of growth would have necessitated a rapid increase in the volume of investment and faster rates of technological innovation. Yet such a strategy was not an easy one for the Ukrainian economy to follow. First, it was not easily amenable to the diffusion of new technology or to the efficient substitution of capital for labour. Second, Ukraine's policy-makers and planners had little say with regard to the planning and management of the large segment of the Ukrainian economy that is administered by all-union and union-republican ministries.[2] Third, maintaining—let alone accelerating—the rate of capital formation was likely to prove difficult.

By 1970, the proportion of Ukrainian national income (utilized) going into gross investment was already too high (27 per cent) and even under very favourable circumstances could not have been raised without impinging on consumption. But conditions were also unfavourable since the slow-down of economic growth made this transfer of resources to capital formation even more difficult. In addition, new claims on investment resources emerged from several quarters. The need to replace depleted sources of energy, minerals and water called for highly capital-intensive projects. The emphasis on preservation of environment placed new demands on investment resources in Ukraine, as it did in other industrial countries. Finally, there was also an expensive claim from the agricultural sector. The crop failures of 1963, 1965, 1967 and 1969 dramatically demonstrated the need to assign greater resources and investment funds to agriculture in the 1970s. A concerted programme aimed at achieving a dependable and steadily rising production of crops and animal products was adopted. This programme included investment in branches of the economy supportive of agriculture. In fact, investment in the agro-industrial sector proved to be a major claimant on the republic's investment resources, accounting for 27 per cent gross investment in the 1970s.

By 1970, it became apparent that the 1965 economic reform had not improved the efficiency of resource utilization in Ukraine. It was in this setting that the Ukrainian economy embarked on its Ninth Five-Year Plan.

Economic Growth

The results of the Ninth Five-Year Plan were disappointing. The overall target for economic growth was not met and there were large shortfalls in a number of important economic sectors. The average annual growth of the total income produced (a Soviet economic concept) in 1971–5 was 4.6 per cent, as opposed to the 6.5–6.8 per cent figure foreseen in the plan. Agricultural production, measured in average annual gross value terms, increased by 15 per cent in the same period, whereas the plan had called for a 20 per cent increase. Total industrial output came close to meeting the objectives set by the Ninth Five-Year Plan—7.1 per cent average annual growth as compared with the planned 7.4 per cent figure. However, despite repeated promises that the consumer goods industries would develop more rapidly than the producer goods sector, the results showed the reverse was still the case. Consumer goods production rose by 6.0 per cent on an average annual basis as against the 7.3 per cent target (see Table 1).

TABLE 1 The Economy of Ukraine, 1975–80: Plan Targets and Actual Performance

Sector	Eighth Five-Year Plan 1970 Results (1965 = 100)	Ninth Five-Year Plan 1975		Tenth Five-Year Plan 1980	
		1975 Plan Targets (1970 = 100)	1976 Plan Results (1970 = 100)	1980 Plan Targets (1975 = 100)	1980 Plan Results (1975 = 100)
National Income Produced[a]	138	137–139	125	122–125	118
Civilian Employment	111	n/a	108	n/a	105
Workers and White-collar staff	121	n/a	113	n/a	109
Fixed capital stock	139	n/a	140	n/a	133[b]
Fixed capital stock (productive only)	147	n/a	147	n/a	143
Investment, gross fixed[a]	139	138	137	116	120
Industry:					
Gross output	150	143	141	130–34	122
Gross output, producers' goods	148	143	145	137	126[b]
Gross output, consumers' goods	155	142	134	124	119[b]
Ingot steel produced	126	116	114	109–115	102
Electricity produced	145	145	141	130	121
Fixed capital stock (productive only)	149	n/a	146	n/a	139[b]
Workers and White-collar staff	120	n/a	109	n/a	109
Capital/person employed	125	n/a	136	n/a	128
Output/capital	100	n/a	96	n/a	87
Labour productivity	128	132	129	128	112

Agriculture:				
Gross value of output[a]	117	115	111–114	108
Grain output[a]	114	120	115–120	108
Fixed capital stock (productive only)	137	145	n/a	144[b]
Labour force (socialized sector only)	90	96	n/a	90[b]
Labour productivity (socialized sector only)	126	127	128	115[b]
Average money wage or salary	123	116	118–120	116
Real income per capita	132	120	n/a	117
Retail sales, state and co-operative (in current rubles)	148	134	126–127.5	125

n/a: not available

Figures in italics are extrapolations or computations by the author

[a] Ratio of investment totals or of average annual output for the five-year periods ending in the stated period.

[b] Extrapolation from 1976–9

SOURCE: *Nar. hosp. 1970*; *Nar. hosp. 1975*; *Pravda Ukrainy*, 30 January 1981; P. Rozenko, "Piatiletnii plan razvitiia narodnogo khoziaistva Ukrainskoi SSR v 1971–1975 gg." in *Ekonomika Sovetskoi Ukrainy*, no. 1 (1972): 4–9; O. S. Singaevskii, "Desiataia piatiletka Sovetskoi Ukrainy," *Ekonomika Sovetskoi Ukrainy*, no. 12 (1976): 1–12.

Ukraine's Tenth Five-Year Plan (1976–80), in terms of both targeted and attained growth rates, was considerably more cautious than its predecessor—a reflection of both long-term retardation in the growth of the republic's economy and of persistent agricultural setbacks. This becomes evident if we compare the results for 1976–80 with the targets for that period and the results achieved in 1971–5. Thus, the total national income produced in 1980 was 18 per cent higher than in 1975. The plan had called for a 22-25 per cent gain, but even in the 1971–5 period, the total gain had been 25 per cent. Similarly between 1976–80, total industrial output grew by 22 per cent, a poor showing when compared with the 42 per cent growth of 1971–5, and well below the 30–34 per cent figure the planners had called for. Agricultural output between 1976–80 increased by a mere 8 per cent, as compared with the 15 per cent growth of the 1971–5 period. The comparable figures for consumer goods production were 19 and 34 per cent (see Table 1).

In the mid-1970s the gross fixed investment of the Ukrainian economy increased only by 20 per cent in the tenth five-year period as compared with the 37–39 per cent increases reported in each of the two preceding five-year plans. This decline interacted with the reduction in the growth of employment and forced the authorities to adjust to a more modest pace of development. Moreover, these official data probably exaggerate the growth rates and, therefore, do not reveal the full scope of the underfulfillment of the Ninth and Tenth Five-Year Plans. Western analysts have found that official statistics in both the USSR and Ukraine suffer from serious deficiencies.[3] The national income statistics for Ukraine are certainly inflated by at least one percentage point per year, because the price index understates the real increases in prices.

Industry

The growth rates of industrial output, as cited in Soviet reports, are also overestimated. This can be confirmed from an examination of data on planned and claimed output of energy and basic industrial materials during the ninth and tenth plan period (see Table 2). The figures for 1971–5 show that while output of electricity, coal, ingot steel, mineral fertilizers and cement each came within a few percentage points of their respective targets, or actually reached them, the output of other industrial materials—oil, steel pipes, chemical fibres and fabrics fell considerably short. Growth in output of energy and major industrial materials slowed appreciably in the 1976–80 period. Moreover, only one of the 1976–80 plan targets was met.

Finished goods fared poorly, despite the high priority accorded them in the 1970s. This was true of machinery, synthetics and plastics, processed

Ukraine After Shelest

TABLE 2 Physical Output of Basic Industrial Products in Ukraine: 1970–80

Product	1970	1975 (plan)	1975 (actual)	1980 (plan)	1980 (actual)
Electricity (bill. kw)	138	198.5	194	253	236
Coal (mill. tons)	207	217.4	216	226–229	197
Oil (mill. tons)	13.9	17.5	12.8	8.6	8.3
Ingot, steel (mill. tons)	46.6	55.6	53.1	58–61	53.7
Steel pipes (mill. tons)	4.5	6.5	5.9	6.3	6.3
Mineral fertilizers (gross. mill. tons)	11.5	16.4	18.3	24.4	19.7
Cement (mill. tons)	17.3	21.5	22.4	25.3	23.6
Chemical fibres (thous. tons)	65.3	150	129	187–193	161
Fabrics (mill. sq. meters)	453	825	742	1030	917

Figures in italics are estimates by the author

SOURCE: As per Table 1.

food, soft goods and major consumer durables. Official claims of output growth in these industrial branches have disguised the price increases.[4] For example, plants introduced "new" and more expensive products which replaced virtually identical older cheaper products. As R. Senkiw has demonstrated, the official index of industrial output for Ukraine differs more from objective Western calculations of the index than is the case for the USSR as a whole.[5]

In order to offset the marked slowdown in the growth of the labour force and of gross investment, which the planners foresaw affecting Ukrainian industry in the 1980s, both the ninth and tenth plans emphasized as the key objectives greater efficiency in resource use, a higher quality of producers' and consumers' goods, and more rapid diffusion of technical progress. Unfortunately, neither central nor republican industrial planners could develop the necessary economic or administrative levers to encourage qualitative or efficient production. The diffusion of new technology remained too slow, and the machinery produced was frequently obsolete and very expensive. Often the product mix and the goods that were delivered did not conform to the users' requirements. Ukrainian decision-makers and planners, in the face of hyper-centralization, could do little to encourage managers to be more economical in the use of resources. Industrial enterprises were wasting fuel, metal, timber and other key materials. Since the net result of this practice was an increase in both volume output and labour productivity, managers and workers were actually rewarded for wasting resources through the system of success indicators and incentives. Several half-hearted attempts to redress this economic anomaly proved unsuccessful with the result that production costs rose steadily. Evidence of this can be seen in the fall in profitability of the republic's industry from 21.8 per cent in 1970 to 13.3 per cent in 1978.[6] The growth, quality and efficiency of Ukrainian industry would have improved markedly had the system overcome its resistance to change and innovation.

Agriculture

Agriculture remained the least efficient sector of the Ukrainian economy throughout the 1970s. There was, however, some progress. In the latter part of the decade, the agricultural sector became more flexible in its response to adverse changes of weather and soil conditions. There were larger yields per hectare in certain key commodities (see Table 3). These gains, however, were achieved at an excessively high cost: a substantial increase in inputs, investments and subsidies (Tables 4 and 5). Over the past decade, agriculture absorbed 27 per cent of the total investment into the Ukrainian economy. This does not include the vast subsidies for livestock products because of the relative cheapness of meat in the urban retail network (meat prices have not changed substantially since the beginning of the 1960s). The greater degree of mechanization, extensive use of chemicals and large-scale land improvement—three main components of Ukrainian agricultural policy in the 1970s—placed a new strain on the planning of industrial supplies and services.

Because of the many inadequacies of the economic mechanism and the system of incentives, the cost of providing industrial supplies and services escalated. In the meantime, mechanization was still not fully implemented, and moreover was un-integrated and of poor quality. Labour was not used efficiently, and the agricultural labour force seemed unwilling to work harder at peak periods. As a result, the Ukrainian leadership had to recruit labour from cities to help with the harvest, thereby disrupting industry and education.[7] There was also a chronic shortage of skilled manpower in rural areas, adversely affecting the maintenance and repair of machinery and equipment. Although fertilizer was supplied much more abundantly than in the 1960s, sizable amounts were either misapplied or simply wasted owing to backward agro-technology, and poor facilities in spreading and storaging. Similarly, a sizable proportion of vegetables, fruits and other perishables that were produced failed to reach consumers because of losses caused by inadequate packaging, shipping and storaging. State and collective farms remained too large, resulting in significant diseconomies of scale and intricate management problems. Persistent interference by party officials and a swollen agricultural bureaucracy further complicated the tasks of farm management and contributed to the deterioration of Ukrainian farming performance. Gross agricultural output and production of grain failed to meet expectations throughout most of the 1970s, including the years blessed with good growing conditions (see Table 1). The livestock sector, according to published data, met production targets in the 1970s. (The performance of the state livestock sector appears to have been overstated, since a large part of its registered production consisted of private animal holdings.) The attainment of the targets was very costly in terms of feed inputs. The development of the Ukrainian livestock sector has relied heavily on increasing feed supplies, and has failed to tap the immense potential offered by improving feed efficiency. In beef production in 1963–77, for instance, the feed input per unit stagnated at the 1962 level.[8] Actual raw protein levels per feed unit were well below the norms, and there has been no perceptible improvement since the mid-1960s. Despite the large increase in fodder consumption, reports suggest that the overall protein deficiency for Ukrainian livestock remained significant.[9]

Obviously, not all these failures and weaknesses were connected with the collectivized and centrally-planned nature of the Ukrainian agriculture. Climate and soil are natural handicaps. The low quality of farm equipment

TABLE 3 Ukraine: Yields of Major Crops (cwt/ha),[a] 1965–79

Year	Winter wheat	Winter rye	Spring Barley	Oats	Maize	Sugar beets	Sunflowers	Potatoes	Vegetables	Maize fodder
1965	21.3	13.2	17.4	15.3	26.9	235	14.7	86	112	132
1966	24.8	12.5	18.9	17.2	26.4	222	15.8	104	114	131
1967	23.1	11.6	17.6	17.0	26.3	257	16.6	96	120	125
1968	20.5	12.4	15.8	13.6	26.4	330	15.8	110	125	119
1969	23.5	13.5	22.6	18.8	30.3	245	18.2	89	114	166
1970	26.0	14.1	24.5	20.8	27.9	280	15.4	99	120	130
1971	29.9	18.8	22.1	18.3	26.9	279	15.8	123	125	150
1972	25.5	15.9	19.2	15.4	22.7	293	13.6	116	118	153
1973	31.9	20.8	26.7	23.8	35.1	279	18.1	116	146	190
1974	31.7	20.0	26.9	22.1	29.1	274	17.3	110	138	176
1975	22.9	14.7	18.3	13.2	24.5	217	14.1	88	116	132
1976	31.1	19.4	29.1	22.7	28.6	345	12.3	138	160	187
1977	31.9	17.9	24.7	21.0	29.5	310	15.7	110	134	201
1978	35.2	20.6	24.7	23.0	32.0	310	14.3	140	161	180
1979	25.8	16.7	18.3	13.5	27.8	263	16.0	135	141	165

[a] hundredweight (100 kilogrammes) per hectare.

SOURCE: *Nar. hosp. 1969* (Kiev 1970), 208–9; *Nar. hosp. 1975*, 194–5; *Nar. hosp. 1979*, 142–3.

TABLE 4 **Ukraine: Main Industrial Deliveries to Agriculture**

Goods (thousands)	1965	1970	1975	1980
Tractors	39.5	45.7	58.6	49.0
Grain Combines	8.9	9.8	10.6	13.0
Trucks and specialized vehicles	11.3	25.0	45.4	44.0
Fertilizer (million gross tons)	5.4	9.4	15.7	16.0

SOURCE: *Nar. hosp. 1979*, 130, 148; *Pravda Ukrainy*, 30 January 1981.

TABLE 5   **Ukraine: Agricultural Investment: 1966–80**
            (in 1000 million rubles)

	1966–80	1971–5	1976–80
Total investment in agriculture	14.0	21.3	25.5
Productive investment only	11.9	19.2	23.0
Per cent of total investment in Ukraine:			
going into agriculture	24.4	27.1	27.1
going into productive agriculture	20.7	24.5	24.5

SOURCE: *Nar. hosp. 1979*, 204–5; *Pravda Ukrainy*, 30 January 1981.

and chronic shortages of spare parts, fertilizer-spreaders, etc., are caused by inadequacies in industry, not agriculture. Nevertheless, it is evident that the institutional character of Ukrainian agriculture contributed to the failures.

First, the wide diversity of natural conditions and complex interrelationships within an agricultural system are not easy to plan under the best of circumstances. Ukrainian farms, subject to onerous micro-economic planning and ponderous control from the party-state machine, offered little scope for individual or group initiative. Detailed instructions from the centre on the delivery plans, timing of sowing and harvesting, etc., narrowed managerial responsiblity, impeded rational specialization, interfered with crop rotation schemes and ignored the availability in each farm of labour and equipment. A large volume could be filled with examples, published in the official press, of ill-thought-out campaigns forced on Ukrainian farms by party and state officials. True, during the 1970s, unlike the preceding decades, more consideration was given to the diversity of farming conditions in Ukraine. But farm management remained subject to detailed instructions from above with concomitant negative effects. Excessive centralization and interference from the centre presents an even more formidable obstacle when it comes to planning and organizing efficient farming than it does in industry, because the variety of conditions of production is much greater in agriculture.

Second, the Ukrainian state and collective farms themselves suffered from diseconomies of scale. During the past decade they remained too large and too diversified to be run efficiently in the absence of decentralized management and flexible planning. Tables 6 and 7 give an idea of the scale of operating units and show that by 1979, although the average state farm and collective farm had about the same amount of arable land and livestock, they differed in the size of their work force and the availability of machinery. Data also indicate that collective farms increased their land area, livestock herd and work force. These farms, however, are usually based upon several villages connected by poor roads. Most farms had a diversified crop and livestock production structure. The management of these large and mixed farms found it difficult to stimulate efficient work because of the tenuous link between the renumeration of individual agricultural workers and final output.

TABLE 6 Ukraine: Average State Farm, 1965–79

	1965	1970	1975	1979
Workers and white-collar staff	714	676	691	669
Arable land (hectares)	4,180	3,738	3,689	3,422
Tractors (thousands)	42	40	45	48
Trucks (″)	27	27	30	33
Cattle (″)	2,085	1,931	2,212	2,281
Pigs (″)	1,564	1,558	1,361	1,616
Sheep and goats (″)	1,117	1,059	1,078	951

SOURCE: *Nar. hosp. 1979*, 166–7.

TABLE 7 Ukraine: Average Collective Farm, 1965–79

	1965	1970	1975	1979
Households	555	554	630	655
Arable land (hectares)	2,700	2,600	3,200	3,400
Trucks (thousands)	12	15	20	22
Tractors (″)	18	23	33	37
Cattle (″)	1,369	1,469	2,023	2,304
Pigs (″)	1,085	1,264	1,260	1,532
Sheep and goats (″)	681	703	864	932

SOURCE: *Nar. hosp. 1979*, 160–1.

The fact that advanced capitalist countries have few farms of similar size to the typical Ukrainian state or collective farm is an indication that diminishing return on economies of scale has become entrenched in Ukrainian farming. There are, of course, farms as big as those of Ukraine in the United States, Canada and Australia. But unlike the Ukrainian farm, these specialize more narrowly and employ less labour. The solution to the problems of diseconomies of scale in Ukrainian agriculture lies in increasing efficient specialization and delegating authority and decision-making to the operating units (the brigade, the team). Furthermore, these problem areas are intertwined with many others. The poor integration of agriculture with the rest of the economy, faulty pricing policies and inflexible planning are major factors contributing to the inefficiency of agricultural specialization in Ukraine. Perhaps the most important is the entire ethos of Soviet directive planning and centralized management that stands in contrast to what is really needed: small autonomous teams in agriculture. A brief look at Ukrainian agricultural policies confirms this.

Since the early 1970s, the party has encouraged "state-collective farm co-operation and agro-industrial integration," in an attempt to link agriculture with industry. Pooling resources, it argued, would result in greater specialization, technical efficiency, and more reliable supplies of industrial inputs and services to agriculture.[10] But at the same time, the party tended to respond to economic problems by tightening discipline, and by attempting a more efficient operation of the centralized planning system, rather than by decentralization measures. Not surprisingly, the solutions devised and implemented throughout the 1970s, despite the favourable publicity they received, did not improve the situation in Ukrainian agriculture.

Third, existing practices in setting prices, incomes and incentives in socialized agriculture proved to be extremely disadvantageous to achieving sustained gains in efficiency and productivity by that sector.

In theory, agricultural prices established by central planners should enable the collective and state farms to decide which products to produce, in what amount, and of what quality. The actual price-setting practice in Soviet-type agriculture, however, has long digressed from the theoretical principles on which it is supposedly based. In spite of agricultural price changes in the late 1960s and during the 1970s, prices did not adapt to the diversity of farming conditions in Ukraine. Academician I. I. Lukinov for example harshly criticized the existing regional variations in grain prices which failed to stimulate efficiency and rational specialization in crop production in the republic.[11] More recently, Ukrainian livestock experts have referred to the quite unsatisfactory situation in the regional variation of procurement and selling prices, as well as the profitability rate in the livestock sector.[12]

Agricultural economists have estimated that, based on existing production costs, a sustained growth in farming output requires a profit margin of not less than 40 per cent.[13] Ukrainian collective and state farms had never reached such an overall profit margin. In fact, the average annual profit margin of collective farms declined from 33.3 per cent in 1966–70 to 15.8 per cent in 1976–9,[14] and for Ukrainian agriculture as a whole, the inter-regional disparities in profitability rates increased during 1971–7.[15] Planned agricultural pricing policies have failed to improve economic incentives for farming in diverse natural conditions.

Income and incentives in socialized agriculture also failed to enhance the efficiency of production throughout the 1970s. Admittedly, the incomes of Ukraine's agricultural labour force were raised substantially in the 1960s. However, improvements in the level of pay appear to have played little role in stimulating efficient work and rectifying serious defects in the use of labour and material incentives. Once again at the root of the problem was the centralization of decision-making and the size of the farm. Large farms without decentralized authority have proved incapable of instituting a rational system of incentives for labour and linking reward with final outcome, since tasks are divided and rewards depend mainly on piece-rate payments and on bonuses related to quantity. According to this incentive scheme, tractor drivers, for example, are paid on the basis of the number of hectares ploughed and also for the amount of fuel saved, rather than on the basis of the actual yield. This practice encourages shallow ploughing which often results in low yields. In general the emphasis on quantity and individual operations in the remuneration of the agricultural labour force reduces the quality, and in the final analysis, the actual output of farms.

On Ukraine's large farms, agricultural workers have little sense of responsibility for the final outcome. Managers and planners confront a labour force unwilling to make extra effort during the harvest season, even though this was formerly a tradition of peasant life. This drastic change in the peasantry's attitude came as a result of the persistent failure of the party-state machinery to harness local initiative, and to become more spontaneous and flexible; to adapt policies to local conditions and above all to the interests of the peasants themselves by bringing the unit of decision-making closer to them, in short by decentralizing and democratizing the large farms. Formally, of course, there is a link between farm management and peasantry. According to the Collective Farm Charter, management is elected and accountable to the members. But the enduring practice of party appointment of these officials long ago severed the link between farm managers and their supposed "electorate." As surveys indicate, the subordination of peasants to bosses and a work routine over which they have no control is partially responsible for the large-scale migration of the younger and more skilled villagers to the towns and for the unfavourable structure of agricultural manpower in Ukraine.[16]

TABLE 8 Ukraine: Main Agricultural Products in the Personal Sector, 1971–9 (million tons)

	1971	1972	1973	1974	1975	1971–5 Average Annual	1976	1977	1978	1979	1976–9 Average Annual
Meat	1.1	1.2	1.1	1.2	1.2	1.2	1.0	1.1	1.1	1.2	1.1
Milk	6.1	6.1	6.1	6.2	6.0	6.1	5.5	6.0	6.0	5.9	5.85
Eggs (mill. units)	5.8	5.8	5.7	5.9	5.8	5.8	5.1	5.6	5.9	5.8	5.6
Potatoes	15.1	14.3	14.6	14.3	11.1	13.9	15.8	12.4	15.9	14.9	14.75
Vegetables	1.9	1.8	2.1	1.8	1.6	1.8	2.0	1.8	2.0	1.8	1.9
Fruits and berries (mill. tons)	1.5	1.0	1.8	1.3	1.3	1.4	1.7	2.2	1.2	2.2	1.8
Grapes	0.18	0.17	0.22	0.20	0.20	0.19	0.15	0.12	0.22	0.22	0.18

SOURCE: *Nar. hosp. 1971*, 184, 216; *Nar. hosp. 1972*, 234, 275; *Nar. hosp. 1973*, 224, 264; *Nar. hosp. 1974*, 242; *Nar. hosp. 1975*, 206, 246; *Nar. hosp. 1977*, 166, 179; *Nar. hosp. 1978*, 134, 146; *Nar. hosp. 1979*, 134, 146; *Iubileinyi statisticheskii sbornik*, 182, 191.

Finally, throughout the 1970s, about 30 per cent of the Ukrainian gross agricultural output came from non-socialized farming. This term encompasses all collective and state farmers, and many other state employees cultivating small allotments (personal household plots) and looking after privately-owned livestock. Personal household plots accounted for one-fourth of the total income of collective farmers and also represented a significant part of the income of state farm workers.[17] On the other hand, the marketed produce from personal plots played an increasingly important role in meeting consumer demand for food. Because of the growth of incomes, especially in families of low- and middle-income brackets, the demand for meat, milk, vegetables and fruit grew faster than their production in the socialized farming sector. According to Ukrainian analysts, since the mid-1970s the share of the non-socialized sector in the total marketed output has been steadily increasing.[18] At the same time, the Soviet authorities' ideological distaste for private economic activity and the meagre allocation of resources to this sector prevented non-socialized Ukrainian agriculture from operating at an optimal level on a modernized technical basis. Labour in this sector was totally non-mechanized and the owners of livestock faced great difficulties in obtaining fodder. The private sector also experienced difficulties and wasted much time in selling products on the free market because of poor roads, shortages of vehicles, and poorly developed marketing services.

Unlike the socialized agriculture sector, whose annual output has varied enormously according to climatic conditions, the personal household plots have largely avoided annual variations in output (see Tables 8 and 9). Official statistics, however, understate the actual performance of the non-socialized sector through the reporting practices of state and collective farms.[19] Sizable quantities of livestock products allegedly produced by these farms were in fact purchased from the private sector. Such transactions, however, did not entail large economic losses for the owners of the private livestock since the procurement prices on livestock produce compared favourably with the collective-farm market prices.

The problems outlined above indicate that despite the high priority

TABLE 9 Ukraine: Private Livestock (1 January, million heads)

	1966	1971	1976	1980
Cows	3.4	3.1	2.8	2.6
Pigs	5.8	5.6	3.8	4.4
Sheep and goats	1.3	0.8	0.6	0.6
Poultry	89.9	98.3	90.8	102.4[a]
Rabbits	4.7	5.8	8.3	12.6[a]

[a] denotes data for 1979.

SOURCE: *Nar. hosp. 1979*, 153–4; *Nar. hosp. 1978*, 144.

The problems outlined above indicate that despite the high priority assigned to development of the Ukrainian socialized agriculture throughout the 1970s, sustained and efficient growth has not yet been attained. Far from becoming a source of revenue, the sector has been a vast burden on the rest of the Ukrainian economy. All the indications are that greater dynamism in Ukrainian farming will be impossible to achieve without far-reaching economic reforms.

Capital

A major source of Ukrainian economic growth has been expansion of capital stock. In the last ten years, capital inputs have increased much faster than labour inputs (see Table 1). These investments have absorbed about a quarter of the republic's total national income. Though Ukraine has met the planned volume of gross fixed investment in terms of rubles, it is unlikely that the target for the physical volume of capital formation was achieved. As in previous periods, the investment programmes of the 1970s have not been satisfactorily balanced with the material and labour resources necessary for their implementation. We have already seriously questioned the attainment of the physical output targets for machinery and metal products, the main suppliers of investment goods. The chronic shortage of investment goods corroborates this phenomenon. The achievement of the overall target for gross fixed investment, in ruble terms, was facilitated by persistent cost overruns, a problem that has attracted much attention from Ukrainian economists and officials. According to estimates by the Ukrainian Gosplan Economic Research Institute, a significant number of projects have spent between 25 to 50 per cent more than originally envisaged in the cost estimates.[20] During the 1970s, there persisted the tendency to start too many projects which could not be finished for lack of resources. Commands were then given to complete only the most important projects, which caused the others to remain unfinished for a period of nine to eleven years, thus multiplying the number of bottlenecks. In the 1970s, the volume of unfinished construction amounted to 75 per cent of total annual state investment and construction took twice as long as originally planned.[21] The perennial campaigns to cut construction delays and reduce the number of unfinished construction projects have failed repeatedly.

Since the end of the 1960s, it has become evident that the already high share of investment in the national income could not be boosted significantly because of the negative repercussions for consumption and the republic's contribution to the federal budget. Hence, Ukrainian planners focused on ways of increasing the efficiency of investment and raising the capital-output ratio in the Ukrainian economy. However, the various investment problems proved to be so deep-rooted and persistent that planners could not cope with them, thus capital productivity did not improve in the 1970s. Indeed, according to estimates, the capital-output ratios for all productive sectors of the Ukrainian economy declined throughout the decade (see Table 10).

TABLE 10 Ukraine: Capital-Output Ratios by Sector (1965=100)

Sector	National income (net product) per ruble of fixed capital stock		
	1970	1975	1977
All productive sectors	90.7	77.6	75.6
Industry	115.9	112.8	108.7
Construction	78.2	58.9	52.1
Agriculture	66.4	37.7	42.1
Transport and communication	99.7	97.6	90.9
Trade	81.2	78.7	79.4

SOURCE: A. S. Emelianov, *Obshchestvennoe proizvodstvo: dinamika, tendentsii, modeli* (Kiev 1980), 134.

Several factors account for the low returns from Ukrainian investments. First, there was the problem of technology. The plants and structures, the machinery and equipment of particular production sectors were outdated and inefficient. Advances in technology can be more quickly put to use in machinery and equipment, since this type of asset is much shorter-lived than buildings and structures. But Ukrainian investments have inclined more toward construction-intensive projects. Although the machinery and equipment proportion in total investment rose from 32 per cent in 1970 to 34 per cent in 1975 and to 38 per cent in 1979, the Ukrainian investment projects have remained among the most construction-intensive.[22] If the analysis is limited to investments into the republican-subordinated economy, then Ukraine's reliance upon construction becomes even more evident—30.8 and 32.9 per cent of total investment respectively for 1975 and 1980.[23]

In part, the low equipment and machinery content observed in Ukrainian investment projects stems from the following reasons. The high investment growth rate; for the higher the rate of investment, the higher the proportion of new, as opposed to replacement, investment. The equipment and machinery component is much lower in the former category. Also, Ukrainian economists and investment experts reported management deficiencies in the construction and design organizations. They noted that the prices quoted for construction projects constantly understated total costs. Furthermore, design organizations were often under pressure from clients to underestimate the overall cost of a project in

order to keep it below a given financial limit and therefore within the
decision-making competence of a particular authority. Design errors
reportedly contributed to inflating costs. Finally, construction firms have
tended to use more expensive methods of work in order to fulfill the plan.
The results of these dubious practices were by no means negligible. As already mentioned, the final cost of most of the Ukrainian investment
projects exceeded initial estimates by 25-50 per cent. At the same time
these "systemic" deficiencies served to reinforce the propensity toward
construction-intensive projects, at the expense of much-needed investment
in equipment and machinery as the main carriers of new technology into
the Ukrainian economy.

Second, the return on investment in the Ukrainian economy was
adversely affected by the low ratio of replacement of obsolescent assets in
net expansive assets. Emphasis on the former type of investment would
raise the machinery and equipment content and promote a more rapid
application of new technologies. The rational course in a period of labour
shortage would be to divert more resources to replacement and
modernization investment thereby reducing cost, as opposed to investment
strategies which expand output. The guidelines of the Ninth Five-Year
Plan emphasized investment in existing plants—64 per cent of all
Ukrainian investment in productive sectors was to be so directed.[24]
However, this proportion included expansion of capacities and capital
repairs. The Ukrainian economist, M. Shkitina, has revealed that the
inclusion of these two components enormously inflates the actual proportion remaining for replacement.[25] His calculations show that only
17 per cent of the total investment into productive sectors was directed
toward replacement during the 1971–4 period (see Table 11). This proportion was 4.5 per cent less than for the 1966–70 period. Moreover, all major
productive sectors of the Ukrainian economy experienced a marked decline
of replacement proportion in investment. In the case of industry, even these
estimates appear to be overstated through the inclusion of regular transfers
of used assets from one industrial branch to another as replacement
investment.[26]

According to economists and planners, understated depreciation rates
and prolonged service lives are primarily responsible for the low
replacement propensity and slow technological advances in Ukrainian industry. The same causes are invariably put forth by analysts to explain the
declining return on investments and fixed assets. A comparison of the U.S.
and Ukrainian scheduled lives for industrial assets illustrates the problem
of the prolonged life-spans of Ukrainian fixed capital (see Table 12). The
assets of the consumer-good and capital-good branches (food, textiles and
apparel, machinery, ferrous metallurgy), in particular, have very low
retirement rates in Ukraine. While the 1975 depreciation rates reduced the

TABLE 11 Ukraine: Reproductive Composition of Investment and New Fixed Assets in Productive Sectors, 1968–74 (in per cent)

| | Years | | | |
| | 1966–70 | | 1971–4 | |
	Replacement	Expansion	Replacement	Expansion
I. Investment:				
All productive sectors	21.1	78.9	16.6	83.4
Industry	19.3	80.7	15.2	84.8
Construction	37.0	63.0	35.6	64.4
Agriculture	26.2	73.8	21.9	78.1
Transportation and Communication	13.1	86.9	11.6	88.4
II. New Fixed Assets:				
All productive sectors	27.0	73.0	25.5	74.5
Industry	20.6	79.4	18.1	81.9
Construction	35.2	64.8	34.3	65.7
Agriculture	47.3	52.7	40.8	59.2
Transportation and Communication	14.0	86.0	11.2	88.8

SOURCE: M. Shkitina, "Sovershenstvovanie vosproizvodstvennoi struktury vvodimykh v deistvie osnovnykh fondov—vazhnyi faktor intensifikatsii," *Ekonomika Sovetskoi Ukrainy*, no. 8 (1976): 38.

service lives of assets and partly corrected the previous policy, encouragement of the rapid incorporation of advanced equipment and technological processes into the Ukrainian economy was still unsatisfactory.[27] Even though the Tenth Five-Year Plan envisaged the increase of the replacement share within the overall strategy of re-equipment and modernization of existing facilities, this goal was not backed by new depreciation policies and other financial incentives. Not only did depreciation and replacement policies fail to reflect the growing obsolescence of equipment and machinery, but the actual retirement rates were reportedly appreciably lower than the plan had foreseen.[28]

The combination of these policies and practices has doubtless enlarged production capacities at great expense since plants with old technology and aged equipment are unlikely to produce cheaply or innovate product mix quickly. In fact, recent Ukrainian reports on rising production costs, stagnating productivity and slow renovating output assortment attribute these phenomena mainly to the planners' failure to orient capital-formation strategies toward technological change through replacement and modernization.[29]

The inefficiencies and weaknesses of investment policies were reflected in the data on the utilization of Ukraine's national income. The Ninth and Tenth Five-Year Plans had envisaged an investment growth rate of 38 and

TABLE 12 Comparative Service Lines of Industrial Assets (in years)

Branch	Ukraine[a]		United States[b]
	1963	1975	1974
Electric power	37	32.5	18–20
Oil and gas	17.7–19.2	17.0–17.3	14–16
Ferrous metals	25.6	22.7	18
Chemicals	27.0	19.6	11
Machinery	26.3	21.3	8–12
Forest products	23.2	16.1	10–16
Construction materials	22.7	19.2	14–20
Textiles and apparel	28.6	23.8	9–14
Food	27.7	23.8	12–18
Total Industry	25.9	21.3	n/a

[a] officially announced schedule;

[b] suggested schedules.

SOURCE: Ukraine—M. Shkitina, "Sovershenstvovanie vosproizvodstvennoi struktury vvodimykh v deistvie fondov—faktor intensifikatsii," *Ekonomika Sovetskoi Ukrainy*, no. 8 (1976): 42; United States—U. S. Department of Treasury, Internal Revenue Service, *Taxation Information on Depreciation*, publication 534.

16 per cent, respectively, and a retail trade turnover rate of 43 and 26–27.5 per cent—a clear priority for consumption. Yet actual developments reveal only a limited shift from investment to consumption. In the ninth plan period, gross capital investment increased by 37 per cent, while retail trade turnover rose by only 34 per cent. By the end of the tenth plan period, investment increased by around 20 per cent, whereas the original plan called for a 16 per cent increase. On the other hand, retail sales were expanding more slowly than planned—25 per cent as against 26–27.5 per cent. Thus, under conditions of slower economic growth and persistent weaknesses in the investment and farming sectors of the Ukrainian economy, the trend of the early 1970s toward a rising share of consumption could not be maintained—on the contrary, under the circumstances, a renewed rise in the investment ratio of the utilized national income was inevitable.

This brings us to the general question of the effect of developments in industry, agriculture and other sectors of the Ukrainian economy during the 1970s on the economic welfare of the population.

Economic Welfare

Throughout the 1970s public discussions and daily propaganda about economic plans both stressed that a new economic strategy had been put into place, one which emphasized an improvement in the standard of living of the Ukrainian population. However, an analysis of the major relevant indicators—such as consumer goods production, money incomes, retail trade turnover and real income per capita—shows that the targets of the Ninth and Tenth Five-Year Plans were far from realized (see Table 1). It is possible to gauge the magnitude of the republic's economic problems from Ukrainian publications.

Table 13 brings together all the main published components of personal incomes and expenditures of the civilian Ukrainian population for 1965 and for the 1970–9 period. On the income side, the wage bill accounted for the bulk of nominal income in Ukraine, and its share remained stable throughout the period (72 per cent). While the wage income of collective farmers rose to 23 per cent over the 1970s, by the end of the decade it accounted for only 10.8 per cent of aggregate institutional income compared with 13.8 per cent in 1970. The published data also show a substantial increase in collective farm dividends per labour day—36.6 per cent between 1970 and 1979.[30] This does not mean, however, that equality in institutional income between collective farms and state employees has been attained, for in 1979, collective farmers' receipts accounted for 13 per cent of the total wage bill, whereas they still represented 18 per cent of the total number of people employed. In 1970, the respective ratios were 16 and 25 per cent, i.e., the income gap was diminishing.

The figures record an increase in cash transfers from the social consumption fund. These almost doubled in value terms and their share in the aggregate income grew from 14.2 to 16.9 per cent between 1970 and 1979. This was the consequence of a variety of social welfare measures adopted during the period by the Ukrainian government. Since the late 1960s the welfare policies have emphasized needs rather than merits for different population groups, that is, they have increased each group's share in the total income provided from social consumption expenditures, as opposed to personal earnings.[31] Among the most significant welfare policies one should mention the extension to collective farms of a state-supported pension scheme with a consequent rise of the minimum sum in 1971, and the extension of the child allowance scheme, announced in 1974, for low-income families. Finally, concerning personal income, Khrushchev's 1957 moratorium on the servicing and repayment of state bonds was abandoned in 1975, and amortization began, absorbing 291 million roubles under the 1979 budget of the Ukrainian SSR.

TABLE 13 Ukraine: Personal Incomes and Expenditures, 1965 and 1970–9 (in billion rubles)

	1965	1970	1971	1972	1973	1974	1975	1976	1977	1978	1979	Increase 1970–9 (per cent)
Average wage[a] (1)	93.9	115.2	118.6	121.9	125.3	128.5	133.5	139.8	142.9	146.2	149.6	29.2
Wage earners[b] (2)	13.4	16.2	16.7	17.1	17.5	17.9	18.4	18.7	19.1	19.5	19.8	22.2
Total wage bill (3)	15.1	22.4	23.8	25.0	26.3	27.6	29.5	31.4	32.7	34.2	35.5	58.5
Income of collective farmers (4)	3.6	4.3	4.6	4.6	4.9	5.0	4.8	5.1	5.3	5.4	5.3	23.3
Social transfer payments[c] (5)	(2.7)	(4.4)	(5.0)	5.5	5.8	6.1	6.8	7.2	7.6	8.0	8.3	88.6
Servicing and repayment of state bonds (6)	0.1	0.2	0.1	0.2	0.2	0.2	0.2	0.2	0.2	0.3	0.3	50.0
Aggregate personal income (7)	21.5	31.3	33.6	35.3	37.3	38.9	41.3	43.9	45.8	47.9	49.4	57.8
Direct taxes (8)	0.8	1.2	1.3	1.3	1.4	1.5	1.6	1.7	1.8	1.9	1.9	58.3
State and Co-operative retail sales (9)	18.5	27.5	29.4	31.4	33.1	34.5	36.9	38.5	40.4	42.1	44.2	60.7
Sales of personal services (10)	0.3	0.8	0.9	1.0	1.1	1.3	1.4	1.5	1.3[d]	1.4	1.5	87.5
Savings bank deposits:												
end-year total (11)	3.5	9.7	10.5	12.2	13.9	16.0	18.6	21.2	24.3	27.7	31.5	224.5
annual increment (12)	0.6	1.0	0.8	1.7	1.7	2.1	2.6	2.6	3.1	3.4	3.8	280.0
Aggregate reported disbursement (13)	20.2	31.3	33.0	35.4	37.3	39.4	42.5	44.3	46.6	48.8	51.4	64.2

Row (3) is the product of rows (1) and (2).

In Row (5) figures in brackets are estimated by using data on the share of cash transfers in social consumption expenditures from A. McAuley, *Economic Welfare in the Soviet Union* (Madison 1979), 262.

Row (7) is the sum of Rows (3), (4), (5), and (6).

Row (12) is the annual increment of Row (11).

Row (13) is the sum of Rows (8), (9), (10), and (12).

[a] Rubles per month, including holiday pay.

[b] Millions at mid-year.

[c] Cash transfers consist of pensions, allowances, and stipends.

[d] Prices on personal services were reduced at the end of 1976.

SOURCE: *Nar. hosp. 1971, 359–60; Nar. hosp. 1972, 411; Nar. hosp. 1973, 400; Nar. hosp. 1974, 293, 416–17; Nar. hosp. 1975, 259, 293, 358, 376, 377, 399, 406, 418, 518, 520; Nar. hosp. 1976, 299–300; Nar. hosp. 1977, 289–90; Nar. hosp. 1978, 216, 217; Nar. hosp. 1979, 160, 221–2, 229–30, 255, 268, 278, 349, 352.*

As already noted, the major portion of personal income is still channelled through wages. The average wage was 149.6 rubles a month in 1979 as compared with 115.2 in 1970. This 30 per cent increase, however, was offset by price increases. Although the official price index was constant throughout the 1970s,[32] it is known that there were significant price increases, especially for non-food products.[33]

A particularly significant change in the wage structure was the sharp decline in the earnings margin between professionals, engineers and technicians, on the one hand, and semi-skilled, and unskilled workers and white-collar staff, on the other. This trend can be ascribed to the lack of trade union pressure to maintain income relativities.

A recent study by G. Schroeder shows that personal nominal incomes per capita have experienced a small relative decline from 97.1 in 1970 to 95.7 in 1978 (USSR = 100), thereby lowering Ukraine's all-union ranking from fifth to sixth in that period, behind the Baltic republics, RSFSR and Belorussia. At the same time, however, the difference in levels of nominal incomes per capita between Ukraine and the most affluent republic—Estonia—has *narrowed* from 36.1 to 31.2 in terms of the national average.[34]

Table 13 presents data on expenditure of the aggregate income. The population's expenditures consisted of direct taxes, retail sales of goods and services (which included indirect taxes) and savings. The unreported types of spending (housing, insurance premiums, and union and party dues), according to budget surveys, have not changed much relative to aggregate disbursements, and therefore accounted for an insignificant and stable part of the total throughout the period. Their omission does not distort an analysis of the major trends in Ukraine's balance of incomes and expenditures.

The most significant trend is the enormous increase in the ratio of savings to income—from 30 per cent in 1970 to 64 per cent in 1979. By the end of 1979 the Ukrainian population held 31.5 billion rubles in savings banks. To examine this phenomenon one must distinguish between the two components of personal savings. The first involves a postponement of the person's current consumption for the sake of a future purchase. Ukrainians, just like Westerners, save for an apartment, a car, a holiday, expensive durables and, especially, for retirement. Certainly, the growth of such savings should not have raised problems of economic imbalances for Ukrainian economic and planning administrators. It is the second component in savings, with its persistent rise on the absolute and relative scales, that has sounded the alarm among planners and economists. These savings represent unsatisfied demand for consumer goods and services, and are directly related to one of the cardinal features of a Soviet-type economy, namely, the chronic imbalance between supply and demand.

I. Birman has justifiably termed such savings as "forced savings," because households are compelled to save, since they cannot buy what they want and are eager to pay for.[35] Soviet Ukrainian economists differ over the proportion of forced savings within the overall savings figure: published estimates range from one-fifth to one-third of the total. What they unanimously agree upon, nonetheless, is that a rising trend in this component of personal savings is having serious repercussions on the Ukrainian economy as a whole in the form of brakes on productivity growth, inflationary pressures in the consumer sector of the economy, and a growing inequality in income distribution.[36] To this list of negative effects one can add the thriving of the second economy (or the black market), by which is meant all production and exchange activities not explicitly taken into account in the planning process or not officially sanctioned as part of the economic system. This phenomenon has been widely recognized, though not fully appreciated, in recent studies by Western Soviet specialists.[37]

Second, the expenditure statistics show no significant relative increase of expenditures on retail goods and services in aggregate reported personal incomes. The respective share of these expenditures grew slightly from 87.8 and 2.6 per cent of aggregate personal incomes in 1970 to 89.5 and 3.0 per cent in 1979. Expenditures on retail goods and services have experienced a considerable absolute rise by 1.6 and 1.9 times, respectively. But in spite of these significant increases in retail and services expenditures, the Ukrainian consumers experienced pronounced shortages in supplies of goods (meat in particular). Although the supply of goods and services and satisfaction of consumer demand improved over the past decade, the demands of Ukraine's population were outpacing the economy's capacity to meet these demands both in quantity and, above all, in the quality and assortment of consumer good supplies.

The tension between consumer demand and the non-availability of goods becomes particularly clear when a comparison of the trend in retail sales (state and co-operative) is made with the trend in savings bank deposits. The 21.8 billion ruble absolute increment in savings over the 1970–9 period was 30 per cent greater than the 16.7 billion ruble increase in retail sales. The savings increment, officially hailed as a sign of the growing prosperity of the population, was in fact evidence of uneasiness and dissatisfaction among Ukrainian consumers. Ukrainian newspapers, such as *Robitnycha hazeta*, published throughout the 1970s many depressing examples of the problems facing consumers. Of far more significance than the discontent, which was manifested even in the heavily censored press, was the fact that in the Ninth and Tenth Five-Year Plans, the growth rates for labour productivity were well below the planners' targets (see Table 1). This cannot be explained solely by shortages of capital and the deficient organization of labour in the Ukrainian economy. Poor labour discipline and blatant lack of interest in raising the quality and efficiency of production are the main reasons behind the feeble growth of labour productivity. The lack of motivation of labour because of shortages of consumer goods poses intractable problems for the Ukrainian economic administration and management. Faced with persistent shortages of consumer goods, workers and white-collar staff see little benefit in producing more. As we have noted, rising money incomes and the failure to stimulate both labour productivity and a more demand-oriented production of consumer goods have led to an alarming growth of "forced savings." This is having grave repercussions on the Ukrainian consumers, such as indifference to the customer's requirements, the second economy, corruption, hoarding and so on. Shortages have grown worse since the early 1970s. This is not because of a decrease in supply; on the contrary, consumption has been rising. But incomes have risen faster, and the increase in prices on certain goods (furniture, jewelry, restaurant meals, gasoline, coffee, alcohol, etc.) have not been sufficient to cope with this "hidden inflation." The retail price of food has remained essentially unaltered for twenty years, although prices on the kolkhoz market have soared.

To summarize: increases in nominal incomes and transfer payments have improved the economic welfare of the Ukrainian population, but at the same time they have widened an inflationary gap, for these increases have been buttressed neither by an adequate supply of consumer goods nor by a rise in labour productivity.

In conclusion, during the 1970s, the Ukrainian economy experienced serious difficulties in adjusting to new constraints on Ukraine's economic development. This assessment of Ukraine's economic performance has emphasized the marked deceleration in growth rates and the failure to meet various quantitative and qualitative targets and demands. Although unlike some Western industrial economies in the grip of recession, the Ukrainian economy *did* experience some growth, the gaps between the plans and performance may indeed amount to a "crisis" in relation to the past rates of growth. The long sought-for breakthrough to an intensive, efficiency-oriented pattern of economic growth has not materialized. These failures can be attributed largely to the inability of the existing economic mechanism to handle the tasks of growth management in the increasingly complex economic setting. This inability is a result of the ambivalence between the Ukrainian economy's need for more decentralization and the highly centralized and bureaucratized Soviet economic system which has retained decision-making authority over the most important sectors of the Ukrainian economy.

Any effort to improve the performance of the Ukrainian economy will have to address itself squarely to this fundamental problem.

Notes

1. O. Alimov, "Rozvytok i vdoskonalennia produktyvnykh syl Ukrainy: dosvid i problemy nauky i praktyky," *Ekonomika Radianskoi Ukraini* 2 (1981).

2. See I. S. Koropeckyj, "Economic Prerogatives," in *The Ukraine within the USSR*, ed. I. S. Koropeckyj (New York 1977).

3. See, for example, V. G. Treml and J. P. Hardt, eds., *Soviet Economic Statistics* (Durham, N.C. 1972); R. Senkiw, *Industrial Production in Ukraine* (Ph.D. dissertation, University of Virginia, 1974).

4. See, for example, *Organizatsiia i planirovanie otraslei narodnogo khoziaistva*, no. 26–7 (1972).

5. Senkiw, *Industrial Production*, 253–7.

6. *Narodne hospodarstvo Ukrainskoi RSR, 1978* (Kiev 1979), 331. (Hereafter *Nar. hosp.*)

7. Ie. A. Iankovska, "Problemy udoskonalennia upravlinnia terytori-alno-haluzevym pererozdilom trudovykh resursiv," *Visnyk Akademii nauk Ukrainskoi RSR*, no. 4 (1980).

8. V. A. Zakharkevich, "Osnovnye faktory, opredeliaiushchie rost proizvodstva goviadiny vo obshchestvennom sektore selskogo khoziaistva," *Organizatsiia i planirovanie otraslei narodnogo khoziaistva*, no. 56 (1979): 132.

9. Ibid., 133.

10. I. I. Lukinov et. al., *Agrarnye problemy razvitogo sotsializma* (Kiev 1979), 83.

11. I. I. Lukinov, *Vosproizvodstvo i tseny* (Moscow 1977), 384–6.

12. Ia. Belousov et. al., "Spetsializatsiia v zhivotnovodstve i ee stimulirovanie," *Ekonomika Sovetskoi Ukrainy*, no. 5 (1979): 41–3.

13. See, for example, Lukinov, *Agrarnye problemy*, 396.

14. A. Onishchenko and A. Tipko, "Problemy razvitiia i sovershenstvovaniia agropromyshlennogo kompleksa Ukrainskoi SSR," *Ekonomika Sovetskoi Ukrainy*, no. 2 (1981): 25.

15. See Lukinov, *Agrarnye problemy*, 342.

16. Ibid., 309.

17. Ibid., 288.

18. Ibid.

19. K. E. Wädekin, "The Public Livestock Draws on Private Animal Holdings," *Radio Liberty*, 466/80, 8 December 1980.

20. A. S. Emelianov, *Obshchestvennoe proizvodstvo: Dinamika, tendentsii, modeli* (Kiev 1980), 114–15.

21. Ibid., 268.

22. *Nar. hosp. 1979*, (Kiev, 1980), 209.

23. O. S. Singaevsii, "Desiataia piatiletka Sovetskoi Ukrainy," *Ekonomika Sovetskoi Ukrainy*, no. 12 (1976): 12. The 1980 figure represents the planned target.

24. Ibid.

25. M. Shkitina, "Sovershenstvovanie vosproizvodstvennoi struktury vvodimykh v deistvie osnovnykh fondov—vazhnyi faktor intensifikatsii," *Ekonomika Sovetskoi Ukrainy*, no. 8 (1976): 37–45.

26. A. Shneiderov, "Vosproizvodstvennye proportsii kapitalnykh vlozhenii," *Voprosy ekonomiki*, no. 8 (1975): 28.

27. Shkitina, "Sovershenstvovanie vosproizvodstvennoi struktury," 43.

28. Emelianov, *Obshchestvennoe proizvodstvo*, 103–4.

29. See I. I. Lukinov, "Problemy ekonomichnoho rozvytku u visimdesiati roky," *Ekonomika Radianskoi Ukrainy*, no. 1 (1981).

30. *Nar. hosp. 1979*, 160.

31. See the discussion of Soviet welfare policies in A. McAuley, *Economic Welfare in the Soviet Union* (Madison 1979), chapter 11.

32. *Nar. hosp. 1979*, 290.

33. See K. Bush, "Soviet Living Standards: Some Salient Data," in *Economic Aspects of Life in the USSR Colloquium* (Brussels 1975).

34. G. E. Schroeder, "Regional living standards," in *Economics of Soviet Regions*, ed. I. S. Koropeckyj and G. E. Schroeder (New York 1981), 120.

35. I. Birman, "The Financial Crisis in the USSR," *Soviet Studies*, no. 1 (January 1980).

36. P. I. Bagrii, *Proportsionalnost i effektivnost vosproizvodstva v usloviiakh razvitogo sotsializma* (Kiev 1980), 353.

37. Useful Western studies on the consumer second economy include G. Grossman, "The Second Economy of the USSR," *Problems of Communism*, no. 5 (September-October 1977); and D. O'Hearn, "The Consumer Second Economy," *Soviet Studies*, no. 2 (April 1980).

Ethno-Demographic Trends in Ukraine in the 1970s

Bohdan Krawchenko

The publication of some of the results of the 1979 census gives us a new insight into ethno-demographic processes in Ukraine in the 1970s. The fact that important sections of the census have not yet been published (and may never be) means that major areas of discussion are not covered in this paper.[1] The information on hand, however, does allow an analysis of changes in the national composition of Ukraine's population and developments in language retention. These are the two themes that will be explored in our paper.

Population

During the 1960s many Ukrainians were alarmed at changes that were occurring in the national composition of the population of Ukraine. Their concern was centred on the unprecedented increase in the number of Russians in the republic. Indeed, between 1959 and 1970, the Russian population of Ukraine grew by slightly over two million or by 28.7 per cent. Ukrainians in the republic, on the other hand, registered a 9.7 per cent increase and as a consequence their share of the republic's population declined from 76.8 to 74.9 per cent in the 1959–70 period.[2] In a number of oblasts—Donetsk, Voroshylovhrad, Odessa—Ukrainians were on the verge of becoming a minority. Throughout Ukraine the large Russian presence was having an adverse effect on the Ukrainians' national self-identification. The size of the Russian population has been one of the most significant variables in explaining the linguistic shift of Ukrainians toward the Russian language. The growth of the Russian population served to weaken and marginalize the institutional infrastructures of Ukrainian national life (schools, theatres, press). Since Russians who settled in

Ukraine clustered in well-paying jobs in urban areas, their influx created a highly competitive environment which hampered the geographical and social mobility of Ukrainians.

The 1970s brought a respite from the ethno-demographic trends of the previous decade only in terms of total numbers. Between 1970 and 1979 Russians increased their population in Ukraine by 9.7 per cent. Because the number of Ukrainians in the republic increased by only 3.4 per cent in the same period, the trend toward a diminution of the Ukrainian majority continued (see Table 1). In one respect, the situation in the 1970s was unprecedented in the postwar years. During the 1970s the increase in the Russian population of Ukraine—1.3 million—was greater in absolute numbers than the growth of the Ukrainian population—1.2 million.

What is the explanation for these ethno-demographic changes? Four factors come to mind: the low rate of natural increase of Ukraine's population, the in-migration of Russians, the out-migration of Ukrainians and the assimilation of Ukrainians to a Russian national identity (Russification). We will briefly examine each in turn.

The rate of natural population growth in Ukraine dropped from 6.4 per 1000 inhabitants in 1970 to 3.4 by 1980, giving the republic the third lowest natural population increase among the fifteen union republics in the USSR. This situation was brought about by two developments. The first was Ukraine's low birth rate, (the second lowest among the union republics in 1980). The crude birth rate (births per 1000 of population, per year) in Ukraine in 1970 was 15.2 and in 1980, 14.8.[3] A more precise picture of the childbearing situation in the republic emerges from an examination of the fertility index (number of births per year per women of childbearing ages, generally considered to be 15–49 years of age). In 1958–9 that index was 70.7, but by 1976–7 it stood at 56.8, a reduction of 20 per cent.[4] The universal employment of women (9 out of every 10 adult women in Ukraine in 1979 were employed), a higher level of education among females, as well as extensive labour outlays by women on domestic chores, poor housing and inadequate day-care and kindergarten facilities, are the major factors which have had a restraining influence on family size.[5] The average family in Ukraine in 1979 consisted of 3.3 people.[6] The birth rates of Ukrainians in the republic were not appreciably higher than those of the Russian residents of Ukraine, despite the higher proportion of urban dwellers among the Russian population.[7] This was because the flight of young people to urban centres and changing life-styles produced a situation in which the Ukrainian village ceased to be a reservoir of population renewal. By 1967 urban and rural birth rates in Ukraine had become equalized and since that date urban birth rates have surpassed those in rural areas everywhere in Ukraine except for some of the western oblasts.[8] Thus the average size of Ukraine's rural family has virtually reached the urban norm: 3.3 per family in rural areas, 3.2 in urban centres in 1979.[9]

TABLE 1 National Composition of the Population of Ukraine, 1959–79[a]

Year	Population	Ukrainians	%	Russians	%	Jews	%	Others	%
1959	41,869,000	32,158,000	76.8	7,091,000	16.9	840,000	2.0	1,779,000	4.3
1970	47,127,000	35,284,000	74.9	9,126,000	19.4	777,000	1.6	1,939,000	4.1
1979	49,609,000[b]	36,489,000	73.6	10,472,000	21.1	634,000	1.3	2,014,000	4.0

[a] Figures are rounded off to the nearest thousand.

[b] Unlike the preceding censuses, the 1979 census gives only the national composition of permanent residents. If temporary residents are added to the total, then the population of Ukraine in 1979 was 49,755,000. If data giving the national composition of the population of Ukraine in 1979 included temporary residents, as it did in 1959 and 1970, then the proportion of Ukrainians would have been slightly less than 73.6 per cent.

SOURCE: *Perepis 1959*, 2: Table 2; *Perepis 1970*, 4: Table 53; *Perepis 1970*, 4: Table 7; *Naselenie SSSR po danym vsesoiuznoi perepisi naseleniia 1979 goda* (Moscow 1980), 28.

The increase in the death rate from 8.8 per 1000 population in 1970 to 11.4 in 1980 was the second factor responsible for Ukraine's low natural population growth. (Ukraine had the third highest death rate among the fifteen union republics.)[10] The higher death rate is in part a natural outcome of an aging population. The number of pensioners as a proportion of Ukraine's total population, for example, grew from 15.7 per cent in 1970 to 18.3 per cent in 1979.[11] But the rise in mortality is also a result of a looming health crisis.[12] The increased death rate for each five-year cohort over the age of 30 during the 1970s is alarming. Between 1970 and 1976 the death rate of those in their forties in Ukraine, for example, rose by 15 per cent.[13] Equally disturbing is the fact that infant mortality is on the rise. Between 1970 and 1974 (the last year statistics were published on this question) infant mortality grew by 12 per cent.[14] Given the unusual Soviet practice of registering infant deaths, the figure was in reality considerably higher.[15] Increased alcoholism among women (related to a more stressful environment) and their heavy reliance on abortion as a method of birth control, as well as poor medical services and the paucity of new drugs, antibiotics in particular, are some of the reasons which account for this tragic turn of events.[16]

Among adults, alcoholism, as well as what two Soviet researchers have called shortcomings in the "work of public health agencies, the disease-prevention system and the struggle against job-related injuries and household accidents" have reduced longevity,[17] possibly by as much as four years.[18] Since the death rate among Ukrainians in Ukraine was higher than that of the republic's Russian population, this offset whatever gains Ukrainians may have made from a slightly higher birth rate.[19] In this situation of demographic parity between Ukrainians and Russians in the republic, it is other processes which play a determinative role in changing the national composition of the republic's population.

The first of these to be considered is Russian in-migration to Ukraine. "In inter-republic population shifts," note two Ukrainian demographers, "the Ukrainian SSR appears as one of the most attractive regions, having propitious natural conditions ... and a high level of industrial development."[20] Throughout the 1970s, migrating Russians increasingly preferred Ukraine over other republics. In absolute numbers, between 1970–9 Ukraine accounted for half the increase in the number of Russians residing outside the RSFSR, 10 per cent more than in the 1959–70 period. But not all regions of Ukraine were equally affected by Russian in-migration. The south and south-eastern regions accounted for 75 per cent of the increase in the Russian population of Ukraine.[21]

Slower overall population growth reduced the size of in-migration to Ukraine during the 1970s. The net in-migration figure for 1959–70 was approximately 500,000. Between 1970–9, on the other hand, net in-migration dropped to roughly 300,000. Net in-migration figures, obtained by the residual technique, represent the total number of people that were added to Ukraine's population other than through natural increase. As such, they do not provide data on population exchange between republics. However, using the same technique, it is possible to calculate the role of in-migration in increasing the size of Ukraine's Russian population. Between 1959–70 the figure thus obtained was 1.2 million and in the 1970–9 period, 840,000.[22] Other authors have estimated that between 1959–70 one million Russians migrated to Ukraine; and a further half a million in the next decade.[23] In a situation where Ukraine's natural population growth is declining and in which the republic's population will actually decrease at the turn of this century, since the death rate will be higher than the birth rate,[24] in-migration, even at a reduced tempo, has emerged as the major factor affecting changes in the national composition of Ukraine's population.

In view of the importance of Russian in-migration to Ukraine, it is worthwhile to consider developments (other than the decline in Russian population growth) which may alter significantly the size of this in-migration in the future. Here the problem of Siberia and the Far East come to the fore. The large Russian in-migration to Ukraine contributed to the development of acute labour shortages in Siberia and the Far East. Indeed, between 1959 and 1972, Siberia experienced a net-migration loss of 1.1 million people.[25] This population movement from a labour-deficit region to locations such as Ukraine which have a more adequate supply of labour, was considered "irrational from the standpoint of society's interests."[26] As a result of measures to improve the standard of living in the RSFSR's remote regions introduced during the Tenth Five-Year Plan (1976–80), some progress was made in reversing this trend. In the second half of the 1970s, the number of people moving to Siberia exceeded the number of those leaving.[27] If this development redirects the movement of the Russian population then it will have an impact not only on the future scope of Russian in-migration to Ukraine, but it may also stem the large out-migration of Ukrainians who, during the 1970s, went to Siberia and the Far East to alleviate the labour shortages.

The out-migration of Ukrainians is a process with a long historical precedent. In recent years, during the 1960s, several hundred thousand Ukrainians were directed by labour recruitment agencies to settle the virgin lands of Central Asia and to work on major projects in the RSFSR. Many who had settled outside their republics in this period, however, returned home. Indeed, between 1959–70, there was a net in-migration of Ukrainians from the RSFSR into Ukraine of more than 300,000.[28] Given that Ukrainian industry, especially in the Dnipropetrovsk, Zaporizhzhia and Donetsk oblasts, began to experience serious shortages of labour,[29] one would have expected less out-migration in the 1970s. In fact, the opposite was the case. Between 1970–9 there was a net out-migration of about 150,000 Ukrainians to the RSFSR.[30] According to a recent study, in the mid-1970s approximately half a million people were leaving Ukraine on an annual basis to work on major industrial projects in the remote regions of the RSFSR.[31] One therefore had a paradoxical situation, in which Ukrainians were out-migrating from a republic whose industry was short of labour whereas Russians were in-migrating in large numbers to Ukraine.

Since the large surplus population of Central Asia, the logical choice for out-migration to the RSFSR's frontier regions, maintained a very low migrational mobility,[32] it appears that in the 1970s that role increasingly fell to Ukraine. As E. A. Ianovskaia has noted, Ukraine "is considered as one of the most important suppliers of workers and specialists for the developing regions of the Urals, the Far East and Kazakhstan through the system of organized migration, organized labour recruitment, and through the placement of graduates of higher educational establishments, tekhnikums, professional schools and the like."[33] According to a recent report, skilled workers and specialists formed an important contingent of those leaving Ukraine.[34] Why, one may ask, did these people not move to Ukraine's south-eastern regions where industry was in much need of personnel? The fact is that the vast majority of job vacancies there involved manual labour in metallurgy and mining using "the shovel, the crowbar and the sledgehammer" and few were willing to work in these "unsatisfactory conditions."[35] The remote regions of the RSFSR at least offered high wages and the possibility of work in one's profession. Obtaining good positions in south-eastern Ukraine, on the other hand, involved competition with Russian immigrants.

Many Ukrainians who migrated to the remote regions of the RSFSR during the 1970s returned home, dissatisfied with climatic conditions, the standard of living and the level of services provided in those regions.[36] Probably many more will be returning in the near future. The results of a 1981 survey of workers in the BAM zone (Baikalo-Amurskaia magistral), the massive railway construction project in the Far East, for example, revealed that 84 per cent of those who had migrated to the zone from Ukraine had no intention of remaining there.[37] Onikienko and Volosozharova claim that Ukraine's increasingly precarious labour supply position may soon limit the scope of out-migration from the republic, and that the out-migration trend of the 1970s will be reversed in the 1980s.[38] If this is so, then it will benefit the Ukrainian nation, which can ill afford a "brain drain" on such a scale. But in the meantime, the number of people leaving for the RSFSR in the 1970s was still greater than the number of people returning, and between 1970 and 1979, the Ukrainian population of Siberia and the Far East increased by 22 per cent.[39]

The number of Ukrainians in the republic was also reduced through their assimilation to a Russian national identity. As S. I. Bruk noted, "As early as 1959, more than two million Ukrainians living in Ukraine identified Russian as their native tongue, and a proportion of them (or their children), might in the intervening period have changed their national self-identity as well."[40] In the process of assimilation, the level of multinationality plays a decisive role. In some regions this level is much higher than in others. (In Western Ukraine it has actually declined, see Table 2.)

A high index of multinationality exerts an influence on assimilation through many avenues. Among the most significant is inter-marriage between Ukrainians and Russians. Over the past forty years marriages between partners of different nationality in Ukraine have increased four-fold.[41] In 1970, 19.8 per cent of all marriages in Ukraine were ethnically mixed marriages; 29.6 per cent in the case of urban marriages, as compared with 7.8 per cent in rural areas.[42] In the city of Kharkiv, which has a large Russian population, the figure rose to 48 per cent.[43] The offspring of ethnically mixed-marriages are not bound by the nationality of their parents. They choose their nationality when applying for the internal passport at the age of 16. Several factors, however, influence their decision. Among the most important is the nationality of the father, especially when the father's nationality coincides with that of the titular nation where the child resides, or when the father's nationality is Russian.[44] Girls, however, are more prone to opt for their mother's nationality than are boys.[45] The "socio-cultural status" of a given nationality also plays an important role in the child's decision.[46] The little evidence at our disposal suggests enormous regional variations in the offspring's choice of nationality. L. Terenteva found that in Cheboksary, capital of the Chuvash ASSR (RSFSR), the overwhelming majority of children whose parents belonged to different nationalities did not opt for the nationality of the titular group (Chuvash) when applying for their passports. In Kiev, on the other hand, half the children of such families gave Ukrainian as their nationality, whereas in Ashkhabad, capital of Turkmenistan, 94 per cent choose a Turkmen identity.[47]

Since immigration beyond the borders of the Soviet Union plays an insignificant role in the demographic process of Ukrainians, it is possible to estimate the rate at which Ukrainians assimilate in the Soviet Union *as a whole.* Comparing the results of the 1959, 1970 and 1979 censuses with the figure that would have resulted from the rate of natural increase, we arrive at a deficit of 670,000 Ukrainians between 1959–70 and a 438,000 deficit between 1970–9. While these figures contain a margin of error, the

TABLE 2 National Composition of Ukraine according to Region, 1926–79[a]

	Year	Total population	Ukrainians	Russians	Others
Donbas	1926	2,982,059	65.4	25.7	8.9
	1959	6,714,220	56.4	37.4	6.2
	1970	7,642,545	53.7	41.0	5.3
	1979	7,937,905	51.6	43.4	5.0
Dnipro	1926	4,315,232	80.8	10.0	9.2
	1959	5,386,561	77.6	17.6	4.8
	1970	6,377,109	74.8	20.8	4.4
	1979	6,830,007	72.8	23.0	4.2
North-East	1926	6,368,755	85.6	10.7	3.7
	1959	5,665,553	81.0	16.2	2.8
	1970	6,037,299	78.5	18.7	2.8
	1979	6,246,113	76.5	20.9	2.6
Central-West	1926	12,606,774	84.0	3.5	12.5
	1959	11,237,522	88.3	6.3	5.4
	1970	11,934,679	87.5	7.7	4.8
	1979	12,301,852	86.5	9.0	4.5
West	1930-1	8,502,400	66.1	0.3	33.6
	1959	7,799,058	87.1	5.2	7.7
	1970	8,754,522	88.2	5.1	6.7
	1979	9,243,677	88.9	5.1	6.0
South	1926	3,735,568	52.5	20.7	26.8
	1959	5,066,132	56.9	30.9	12.2
	1970	6,380,614	55.0	34.0	11.0
	1979	7,073,525	53.5	36.3	10.2

[a] Prewar data were obtained from index cards supplied by Lew Shankowsky and reproduced with his permission. Mr. Shankowsky translated prewar administrative divisions into postwar oblasts.

Ukraine's twenty-five oblasts are regrouped into six major regions following the system used by R. Szporluk, "Russians in Ukraine and the Problems of Ukrainian Identity in the USSR," in *Ukraine in the Seventies*, ed. P. J. Potichnyj, (Oakville 1975), 202. The Donbas consists of two oblasts: Donetsk and Voroshylovhrad; Dnipro: Dnipropetrovsk, Zaporizhzhia and Kirovohrad; North East: Kharkiv, Poltava and Sumy; Central West: Kiev, Chernihiv, Cherkassy, Zhytomyr, Vinnytsia and Khemlnytskyi; West: Lviv, Rivne, Ternopil, Ivano-Frankivsk, Volyn, Transcarpathia; South: Odessa, the Crimea, Kherson and Mykolaiv oblasts.

SOURCE: *Perepis 1959*, 2 Table 54; *Perepis 1970*, 4, Table 8; *Vestnik statistiki*, no. 8 (1980), Table 5.

relationship between the 1959–70 and 1970–9 data is not far off the mark. Thus although the numbers assimilating in the 1970s were still substantial, the rate declined in comparison with the previous decade. This is surprising, since a greater proportion of Ukrainians resided outside the boundaries of their republic and the mother-tongue identification among Ukrainians had also declined.[48] Certainly the data suggest that assimilation is neither a unilinear nor an inevitable process. An examination of language trends in the light of the 1979 census may provide us with deeper insights into this complex social phenomenon.

Language and national identity

The problem of the development of a Ukrainian national identity looms large throughout Ukrainian history, and the urbanization and industrialization of society in recent decades has posed its most formidable challenge to date. However, in discussing trends in this respect, the student of Soviet Ukraine faces the thorny problem of how to measure the strength or weakness of national identity. In other countries, the data base for a study of this question can involve attitudinal studies, and by employing such techniques as preference ratings, inventories of values, rank-order tests, etc., the researcher can obtain a far more refined picture than can be had from language data provided in the census. In the case of Ukraine, with rare exceptions, we must rely solely on language identification for our evolution of developments concerning national self-identity.

But what importance should we attach to language data as an indicator of national self-awareness? National self-awareness is, of course, the most important component of ethnicity; it is distinct from and more enduring than native language. A recent study of ethnic identity formation among urban children in Kiev and Transcarpathia, for example, found that language did not play a significant role in the formation of their Ukrainian national self-identity. The well-springs of national self-consciousness were quite variegated, involving aspects of the material and intellectual culture of Ukrainians.[49] National self-consciousness, moreover, having achieved a definite stage of development, can acquire an independent existence and can have a reciprocal influence on other elements of national identity, such as language. An example of this is found in the examination of ethnic groups in Western Siberia. In that region only 38 per cent of Ukrainians regarded Ukrainian as their mother-tongue and 95 per cent were fluent in Russian. Yet when asked whether they would like their children to be taught Ukrainian in Siberian schools, a surprising two-thirds responded positively to this very sensitive question.[50]

The problem, however, is that the only *measurable* indicator of trends in national self-identification in the Soviet Ukrainian context is language. But one should bear in mind that assimilation is not a linguistic process, but a complete or near complete loss of national self-identity and the full or almost total acceptance of another identity.[51] Linguistic assimilation is, of course, an important step in that process and it is one which proceeds by stages. We can hypothesize what each of these stages represent for national self-identity and, using the census data at our disposal, we can then evaluate what proportion of the Ukrainian population is at a given stage of the linguistic and therefore national assimilation process.

The first linguistic group we can identify among Ukrainians in the 1970 and 1979 censuses are the 'unadapted.' These are Ukrainians who gave Ukrainian as their mother-tongue and did not know Russian. Those who learnt Russian but retained Ukrainian as their mother-tongue we call the 'adapted.' In the light of the 1970 census the majority of children under the age of 10 and adults over the age of 40 belonged to the 'unadapted' group, that is, they were unilingual Ukrainian speakers. (The 1979 census language data by age category have not yet been published, see Table 3.) Persons of working age who fell into this category were engaged predominantly in unskilled labour in urban areas and in the countryside, with a less than average level of education.[52] Their sense of national identity, unlike that of the better educated layers of the Ukrainian population, is not "intellectual or rooted in a set of socio-economic causes" but is "socio-cultural."[53] In their case it is the most visible cultural markers that play a predominant role in determining their national self-consciousness, rather than more abstract notions. At the same time, the unilingual Ukrainians, more than any other segment of the indigenous population have preserved the national traditions and prejudices of that nation. In 1970, 56 per cent of Ukrainians were unadapted. This figure declined to 37.3 per cent in 1979. In 1979 only Western Ukraine showed a (slim) majority of the Ukrainian population as belonging to the unadapted category (see Table 4).

Comparing the 1970 and 1979 census returns, it appears that 6.3 million Ukrainians learnt Russian in the intercensus period, that is, they moved from the unadapted to the adapted category. This large increase must be treated with caution. Both the 1970 and 1979 census data on knowledge of Russian are permeated with obvious falsifications. Nowhere was this more blatant than in the statistics on the number of Uzbeks who knew Russian. Among Uzbeks, Russian-language facility grew, according to official sources, from 1.3 million or 14.5 per cent of the total in 1970, the lowest percentage among the titular nations, to 6.1 million or 49.3 per cent of the total in 1979, a 470 per cent increase which placed them among the most bilingual of nations in the Soviet Union. From *samvydav* sources we know that in Lithuania enumerators were issued instructions to artificially increase the number of Russian speakers for the purposes of the 1979 census.[54] In the case of Ukraine the 1970 and 1979 census data contain a number of anomalies that can best be explained by falsifications analogous to those that occurred in Lithuania.[55] Moreover, the concept of language 'fluency' in the census is imprecise. In Ukraine, what on occasion passes for Russian is *surzyk*, a Ukrainian-Russian argot. Functional unilingualism is certainly more prevalent than the census figures suggest. I. B. Dzafarov, for example, noted that "full bilingualism is a phenomenon which is not very

TABLE 3 **National Identity Data of Ukrainians according to Age Group, 1970[a]**
(percentages)

Age group	Total number	Unadapted	Adapted	Acculturated	Russified
0–10	6,421,117	81	8	2	9
11–15	3,110,766	47	43	6	4
16–19	2,216,506	22	67	7	3
20–29	4,416,398	27	63	7	3
30–39	5,445,649	41	50	7	3
40–49	4,925,905	52	41	4	3
50–59	3,530,416	67	26	4	3
60+	5,168,710	79	16	3	2

[a] Unadapted = unilingual Ukrainian speakers; adapted = Ukrainians who give Ukrainian as their mother-tongue and know Russian; acculturated = Ukrainians who give Russian as their mother-tongue but know Ukrainian; Russified = Ukrainians who give Russian as their mother-tongue and do not know Ukrainian.

SOURCE: Calculated from *Perepis 1970*, 4: Table 33.

TABLE 4 **National Identity Data of Ukrainians according to Region, 1970–9**
(percentages)

		Total Ukrainian	Ukrainians			
	Year	Population	Unadapted	Adapted	Acculturated	Russified
Donbas	1970	4,103,479	30.0	43.4	12.8	13.8
	1979	4,095,268	21.7	44.0	16.9	17.4
Dnipro	1970	4,766,924	49.5	41.4	4.9	4.2
	1979	4,970,126	32.6	55.0	7.0	5.3
North-East	1970	4,739,075	52.3	38.9	4.6	4.2
	1979	4,777,199	23.9	65.3	7.0	3.8
Central-West[a]	1970	9,388,545	69.3	28.8	0.9	0.9
	1979	9,187,741	46.8	50.7	1.5	1.0
Kiev city	1970	1,056,905	20.6	56.9	14.8	7.7
	1979	1,456,000	n/a	n/a	n/a	n/a
West	1970	7,721,898	68.5	30.6	0.6	0.3
	1979	8,216,425	51.6	47.4	0.7	0.3
South[b]	1970	3,026,198	46.5	40.1	6.9	6.4
	1979	3,239,277	33.9	49.0	8.2	8.8
Crimea	1970	480,733	25.6	33.1	11.6	29.7
	1979	547,336	16.6	36.1	12.7	34.6
Ukraine	1970	35,283,857	55.6	35.8	4.3	4.2
	1979	36,488,951	37.3	51.8	5.8	5.1

[a] Does not include the city of Kiev.

[b] Does not include Crimea.

SOURCE: Calculated from *Perepis 1970*, 4: Tables 7 and 8; *Vestnik statistiki*, no. 8 (1980): 64–8.

widespread: those who today have a perfect command of two languages do not represent more than five per cent of all bilingual persons."[56]

Desirable though unilingualism may be from the point of view of the preservation of the traditional Ukrainian 'ethnos,' those persons in this category cannot participate fully in contemporary Soviet Ukrainian life. In the Soviet Ukrainian context, a knowledge of Russian is indispensable for entry into institutions of higher learning, and "is almost mandatory for white-collar staff."[57] Knowing Russian, however, as M. N. Guboglo noted in his study of verbal behaviour, "does not as a general rule ... lead to a switch in conscious ethnic affiliation, or a change in other ethnic determinants."[58] Having declared Ukrainian to be its mother-tongue, the adapted group has indicated that it retains close psychological identification with its nation. In 1970, the majority of young adults belonged to this category (see Table 3). The bearers of a national identity of a modern, industrialized, urbanized and literate society are drawn largely from this group. In 1979, 52 per cent of Ukrainians could be considered 'adapted' (see Table 4).

The third group are those whom we call the 'acculturated' Ukrainians. These are people who have lost their mother-tongue identification but have preserved a knowledge of the Ukrainian language. The "change in mother-tongue identification does not in itself tell us about the state of ethnic indices and the stability of the ethnos.... The paradox lies in the fact that among some Gaguz professional people, for example, the acquisition of the Russian language [as a mother-tongue] has gone hand-in-hand with a rise in ethnic self-awareness."[59] But on the whole, mother-tongue retention, especially given the phrasing of the question in the census questionnaire, is a measure of the person's psychological attitude toward the language.[60] The surrender of the distinctive mother-tongue can be regarded as "evidence of a *tendency* toward a certain ethnic indifference."[61]

Acculturated Ukrainians numbered 1.5 million in 1970 and 2.1 million in 1979. Whereas in the Central-West and Western regions of the republic they represented an insignificant proportion of the population, in Donbas they accounted for 17 per cent of Ukrainians in 1979. (In the intercensus period almost a quarter of the increase in the number of acculturated Ukrainians was accounted for by Donetsk oblast.) In the republic as a whole the proportion of acculturated Ukrainians grew from 4.3 per cent of the total in 1970 to 5.8 per cent in 1979 (see Table 4).

'Russified' Ukrainians make up the final group: those who gave Ukrainian as their nationality, but gave Russian as their mother-tongue and indicated that they did not know the Ukrainian language. They are unilingual Russian speakers. A large number of them are undoubtedly the offspring of mixed marriages. Language identification and language knowledge provides an important shield against changes in national self-identification. In the case of this contingent, such protection is gone and they or their children are more likely to assimilate into a Russian national identity than any other group of Ukrainians.

Russified Ukrainians in 1970 formed 4 per cent of the total number of Ukrainians in the republic and this increased by one percentage point in 1979. Russification appears to be very much a regional phenomenon. In 1979, for example, Ukrainians in Donetsk, Voroshylovhrad and Crimean oblasts, although representing 27 per cent of the total Ukrainian population, accounted for half the number of Russified Ukrainians in the republic (see Table 4).

The maintenance of mother-tongue is, as we have argued, a measure of the person's positive psychological attitude toward the language. The 1959 census provided data on this question, allowing for a comparison over a twenty-year period. Between 1959 and 1979 mother-tongue identification among Ukrainians dropped from 93.5 per cent of the total to 89.1 per cent (see Table 5). In some regions the decline was not only relative, but absolute. In these areas, as the older Ukrainian generation, which has a much higher rate of mother-tongue identification dies, and new cohorts of Ukrainians whose mother-tongue is Russian are added, the decline in mother-tongue identification is not incremental, but proceeds in multiples.

Mother-tongue data point to a slow process of acculturation and Russification in some regions of Ukraine. But when placed in the context of the enormous pressures for Russification that Ukrainians have been subjected to in the past two decades, the data also suggests that the Ukrainian ethos is a good deal more stable than some theorists of the merging of nations would hope. As one of the Soviet Union's leading sociologists recently wrote:

> We must also come to grips with the extraordinary durability of national self-awareness as such. Experience has shown that even when persons of different nationalities begin to speak a single language and even when the traditional distinctiveness of national characteristics fades into the past, people retain a feeling of national identity and a sense of their difference from people of different origins for a long time.... Overcoming national differences is a long and complicated process.[62]

National identity, like assimilation, is not a static state, but rather a dynamic process. The strength or weakness of a national identity is bound up with factors such as the development of national cultural infrastructures (the media, schools) and the central state's toleration of the national message which they may communicate. (For example, among urban adolescents in Kiev, it was found that the Ukrainian-language press, radio and television, played a major role in shaping national self-consciousness.)[63]

TABLE 5   **Mother-Tongue Identification of UKrainians According to Region, 1959–79**

	1959		1970		1979	
	Total giving Ukrainian as mother-tongue	As per cent of total Ukrainian	Total giving Ukrainian as mother-tongue	As per cent of total Ukrainian	Total giving Ukrainian as mother-tongue	As per cent of total Ukrainian
Donbas	3,109,400	82.2	3,011,218	73.4	2,690,287	65.7
Dnipro	3,902,932	93.3	4,336,179	91.0	4,353,271	87.6
North-East	4,287,975	93.4	4,322,541	91.2	4,261,420	89.2
Central-West	9,551,603	96.3	10,034,019	96.1	10,129,330	95.2
West	6,726,710	99.0	7,649,257	99.1	8,134,780	99.0
South	2,493,731	86.5	2,904,146	82.8	2,975,397	78.6
UKRAINE	30,072,360	93.5	32,257,360	91.4	32,493,647	89.1

SOURCE: Tabulated from *Perepis 1959*, 2, Table 54; *Perepis 1970*, 4, Table 8; *Vestnik statistiki*, no. 8 (1980).

The existence of these infrastructures and the content of their message depends, in turn, on the political conjuncture. The 'objective' facts concerning language reflect the political defeat of the Ukrainian party leadership, the intelligentsia and the broad sectors of the public who, in the 1960s, attempted to promote the Ukrainian language.

A strengthening or weakening of national attitudes among the urban, educated sectors of society, is less a function of the prevalence of the traditional distinctive cultural traits of a people, or the level of multinationality, than of the concrete social conditions which affect the social and occupational interests of this group. National "exclusiveness and prejudice" bred by social conditions can be found among all strata of the population, "but they are more characteristic of educated people: their cultural horizons are fairly broad, but their social expectations are always higher, and so they are more often dissatisfied."[64] The crisis in the social mobility of Ukrainians, the failure of Ukrainians to improve their standing among students of higher education, the intelligentsia and white-collar occupations in the 1960s, the highly competitive environment that was created in Ukraine as a result of the large Russian in-migration, was the social backdrop for the recrudescence of Ukrainian nationalism in that decade.[65] We do not yet have the 1979 census data which would allow us to gauge whether or not social opportunities for Ukrainians improved in the 1970s. Given the economic stagnation of recent years, together with a high-rate of Russian in-migration, there is reason to believe that the avenues of social mobility have narrowed still further.

Notes

1. It appears that the Soviet government will not publish a series of volumes on the results of the 1979 population census as was undertaken for previous censuses. See M. Feshbach, "Census Censored," *Problems of Communism* (November-December 1982), 87.

2. *Itogi vsesoiuznoi perepisi naseleniia 1959 goda*, 16 vols. (Moscow, 1962–3) 2: Table 53 (hereafter *Perepis 1959*); *Itogi vsesoiuznoi perepisi naseleniia 1970 goda*, 7 vols. (Moscow, 1972–3), 4: Table 7. (Hereafter *Perepis 1970*.)

3. *Narodnoe khoziaistvo SSSR v 1980 g.* (Moscow 1981), 32–3. (Hereafter *Nar. khoz.*)

4. *Narodne hospodarstvo Ukrainskoi RSR. Iubileinyi statystychnyi shchorichnyk* (Kiev 1977), 20. (Hereafter *Nar. hosp.*)

5. *News from Ukraine*, 30 December 1979; M. Sonin, "Problemy semi i rozhdaemosti v demograficheskoi literature," *Kommunist*, no. 8 (1981): 119–23.

6. *Robitnycha hazeta*, 30 December 1979.

7. L. E. Darskii, "Sotsialno-demograficheskie issledovaniia problem rozhdaemosti," *Sotsiologicheskie issledovaniia*, no. 3 (1979): 12.

8. V. V. Onikienko and V. A. Volosozharova, "Osobennosti demograficheskogo razvitiia Ukrainskoi SSR," in *Regionalnye osobennosti vosproizvodstva i migratsii naseleniia v SSSR* (Moscow 1981), 151.

9. *Nar. hosp. Iubileinyi*, 17; *Robitnycha hazeta*, 30 December 1979.

10. *Nar. hosp. 1980*, 32–3.

11. *Perepis 1970*, 5: Table 10; *Vestnik statistiki*, no. 9 (1982): 80.

12. See the interview with Ukraine's Minister of Public Health in *Literaturnaia gazeta*, 9 December 1981.

13. *Nar. hosp. Iubileinyi*, 20. Soviet statistical handbooks ceased publishing data on mortality according to age group after 1976.

14. *Nar. hosp. 1974*, (Kiev 1975), 18, 21.

15. If the birth is earlier than 28 weeks following conception, or if the newborn is less than 1 kilogramme in weight or 35 centimetres in length or dies within seven days of birth, then it is not included in Soviet mortality statistics. See M. Maksudov, "Some Causes of Rising Mortality in the USSR," *Russia*, no. 4 (1981): 13.

16. Ibid., 4–9; *Literaturnaia gazeta*, 20 December 1978.

17. *Pravda*, 19 June 1981.

18. N. Eberstadt, "The Health Crisis in the USSR," *New York Review of Books*, 19 February 1981, 23.

19. See V. I. Naulko, *Etnichnyi sklad naseleniia Ukrainskoi RSR* (Kiev 1965), Table 14, 85.

20. Onikienko and Volosozharova, "Osobennosti," 154.

21. *Perepis 1970*, 4: Tables 2 and 8; *Vestnik statistiki*, no. 8 (1980): 66–8.

22. This calculation is based on the probable assumption that Russians and Ukrainians in the republic had a rate of natural increase that was close to the republic's norm. Calculated from: *Nar. hosp. 1964* (Kiev 1965), 8, 13; *Nar. hosp. 1973* (Kiev 1974), 7, 17; *Nar. hosp. 1979* (Kiev 1980), 5, 15; *Perepis 1970*, 4: Table 7; *Naselenie SSSR po dannym vsesoiuznoi perepisi naseleniia 1979 goda* (Moscow 1980), 28.

23. S. Bruk, "Natsionalnost i iazyk v perepisi 1970 goda," *Vestnik statistiki*, no. 5 (1972); T. Shabad, "Ethnic Results of the 1979 Soviet Census," *Soviet Geography*, no. 7 (September 1980): 463.

24. V. S. Zhuchenko, V. G. Burlin and V. S. Steshenko, *Demograficheskoe razvitie Ukrainskoi SSR (1959–1970 gg.)* (Kiev 1977), Table 81, 154.

25. S. N. Zhelezko, "Molodezh na BAMe," in *Sovetskaia molodezh. Demograficheskii aspekt* (Moscow 1981), 99.

26. *Pravda*, 19 June 1981.

27. *Pravda*, 11 September 1981.

28. Shabad, "Ethnic Results," 463.

29. See interview with Vitalii Masol, Chairman of Ukraine's State Planning Commission in *News From Ukraine*, no. 39 (September 1980).

30. Shabad, "Ethnic Results," 463.
31. Onikienko and Volosozharova, "Osobennosti," 154.
32. See article by V. Perevedentsev in *Literaturnaia gazeta*, 3 October 1979.
33. E. A. Ianovskaia, "Estestvennoe i mekhanicheskoe dvizheniie naseleniia i problemy ratsionalnogo ispolzovaniia trudovykh resursov Ukrainskoi SSR," in *Regionalnye problemy naseleniia i trudovye resursy SSSR*, ed. V. G. Kostakov and E. L. Manevich (Moscow 1978), 60.
34. Onikienko and Volosozharova, "Osobennosti," 154.
35. *Komsomolskaia pravda*, 17 January 1977.
36. Onikienko and Volosozharova, "Osobennosti," 154.
37. V. Voronov and I. P. Smirnov, "Zakreplenie molodezhi v zone BAMa," *Sotsiologicheskie issledovaniia*, no. 2 (1981): 21.
38. Onikienko and Volosozharova, "Osobennosti," 155.
39. *Perepis 1970*, 4: Table 6; *Vestnik statistiki*, no. 7 (1980): 46–64.
40. S. I. Bruk, "Etnodemograficheskie protsessy v SSSR. Po materialam perepisi 1970 goda," *Sovetskaia etnografiia*, no. 4 (1971): 29.
41. L. V. Chuiko, *Braki i razvody. Demograficheskoe issledovanie na primere Ukrainskoi SSR* (Moscow 1975), 78.
42. *Perepis 1970*, 7: Table 30.
43. Z. Sokolynsky, "Demohrafichni doslidzhennia sotsialistychnoho mista," *Ekonomika Radianskoi Ukrainy*, no. 2 (1969): 89.
44. Iu. V. Arutiunian, L. M. Drobizheva and V. S. Zelenchuk, eds., "A Preliminary Ethnosociological Study of Way of Life," *Soviet Sociology*, no. 2 (1982): 62.
45. I. A. Snezhikova, "K probleme izucheniia etnicheskogo samosoznaniia u detei i iunoshestva (po materialam Kievskoi i Zakarpatskoi oblastei)," *Sovetskaia etnografiia*, no. 1 (1982): 85.
46. V. I. Kozlov, *Natsionalnosti SSSR. Etnodemograficheskii obzor*, 3d ed. (Moscow 1982), 263.
47. V. Horlenko and V. Naulko, "Naukovi sesii etnohrafiv," *Narodna tvorchist ta etnohrafiia*, no. 4 (1969): 108.
48. In 1959, 1970 and 1979, 15.8, 15.5 and 16.1 per cent of the total number of Ukrainians in the USSR resided outside Ukraine in the respective years. In 1959, 87.7 per cent of Ukrainians in the USSR gave Ukrainian as their mother-tongue. In 1970 the figure was 85.7 per cent and in 1979, 82.8 per cent.
49. Snezhikova, "K probleme izucheniia," 84–8.
50. N. A. Tomilov, "Sovremennye ethnicheskie protsessy v iuzhnoi i srednoi polose Zapadnoi Sibiri," *Sovetskaia etnografiia*, no. 4 (1978): 17–18. The question is sensitive because since the abandonment of Ukrainianization policies in the early 1930s, the Ukrainian language has not been taught in schools outside the boundaries of Ukraine, despite the fact that Ukrainians are a sizable minority in the RSFSR. The introduction of Ukrainian-language instruction was raised, albeit unsuccessfully, by the national movement in Ukraine in the 1960s.

51. S. A. Arutiunov, "Bilingvizm i bikulturalizm," *Sovetskaia etnografiia*, no. 2 (1978): 3n.

52. See I. Dzyuba, *Internationalism or Russification?* (New York 1974), 135–6; V. I. Naulko, *Razvitie mezhetnicheskikh sviazei na Ukraine (istoriko-etnograficheskii ocherk)* (Kiev 1975), 146.

53. Iu. V. Arutiunian, "Konkretno-sotsiologicheskoe issledovanie natsionalnykh otnoshenii," *Voprosy istorii*, no. 12 (1969): 135.

54. Enumerators were ordered to register all children over the age of seven, all those who speak even a modicum of Russian, those who had completed secondary or higher education since the Second World War and those who indicated knowledge of a second language other than Russian, as "fluent" speakers of Russian for the purpose of the census. See *Diialoh*, no. 3 (1980): 90–1.

55. The contrast between Ternopil oblast in Western Ukraine and Kirovohrad oblast in the Dnipro region is a case in point. Major industries are located in Kirovohrad oblast, over half its population lives in the urban centres, Ukrainians form 87 per cent of the population and this region has been part of the USSR since its inception. Ternopil, on the other hand, was annexed by the USSR during the Second World War, almost 70 per cent of its population is rural and it is one of the most ethnically homogeneous oblasts in the republic with 97 per cent of its population belonging to the Ukrainian nationality. Yet the percentage of unilingual Ukrainians in Ternopil in 1979 was 48 per cent, equal to that in Kirovohrad. The number of unilingual Ukrainians in Ternopil was undoubtedly higher than the figure given in the census.

56. I. V. Dzafarov, "K voprosu o sushchnosti dvuiazychiia v SSSR," *Sotsiologicheskie issledovaniia*, no. 4 (1980): 44.

57. M. N. Guboglo, "K izucheniiu perspektiv razvitiia dvuiazychiia u narodov SSSR," *Istoriia SSSR*, no. 1 (1978): 38.

58. M. N. Guboglo, "Sotsialno-etnicheskie posledstviia dvuiazychiia," *Sovetskaia etnografiia*, no. 2 (1972): 31.

59. M. N. Guboglo, "Ethnolinguistic Processes in Southern Moldavia," *Soviet Sociology*, no. 3 (1974–5): 50, 55–6n.

60. In the 1959, 1970 and 1979 censuses, the instruction was given that in response to the question of mother-tongue, "the name of that language which the subject regards himself as his native language is to be put down." In 1926, on the other hand, mother-tongue was defined as the "language which the subject knows best or which he usually *speaks*." Thus the definition of the concept shifted direction away from language usage to the psychological attitude of the subject toward the language.

61. *Sotsialnoe i natsionalnoe* (Moscow 1977), 29.

62. L. A. Gordon, "Obshchee v osobennom: sotsiologicheskie ocherki ob Estonii," *Sotsiologicheskie issledovaniia*, no. 4 (1980): 193–4.

63. Snezhikova, "K probleme izucheniia," 86.

64. L. M. Drobizheva, "Mezhlichnostnye natsionalnye otnosheniia: osnovnye cherty i osobennosti," *Sotsiologicheskie issledovaniia*, no. 4 (1982): 40.

65. This theme is developed in B. Krawchenko, *Social Change and National Consciousness in Twentieth Century Ukraine* (forthcoming, Macmillan, London).

Contributors

Bohdan Krawchenko

Research Associate, Canadian Institute of Ukrainian Studies, University of Alberta

Bohdan Nahaylo

Graduate student, London School of Economics and Political Science

Gennady Ozornoy

Graduate student, Institute of Soviet and East European Studies, University of Glasgow

Myroslav Shkandrij

Assistant Professor, Department of Germanic and Slavic Studies, University of Calgary

Roman Solchanyk

Research Analyst for Nationality Affairs, Radio Liberty, Munich